MW01180992

***

Special Acknowledgments

I'd like to thank Carol Sherwood for her help with this book! I truly appreciate the time you took out of your schedule to help me.

CHAPTER ONE

Steens Mountains, Spring 1880

"Thoughts of you keep your memory alive in my heart." Charlotte 'Chancy' Mallory wiped an escaped tear from her dust stained cheek. She balanced on her knees over semi-frozen earth covered with bunches of dew covered grass. With a glassy stare, she gazed long and hard at the cold, gray stone grave markers of her three older brothers. She squeezed the wooden toy she held in her palm. A carved horse which once belonged to the youngest of the three before he went to heaven. The relic was her most treasured possession.

The white picket fence her father had touched up with paint several weeks prior glistened against the new growth of spring grasses surrounding their final resting place. Memories, full of guilt and melancholy for what would never be clouded her heart. Blowing a kiss toward the three separate graves: John Henry, Teddy Joseph, and Wayne Kearney; her attention scanned past the hillside to the engorged, snow melted river below. The water's fluid rush over the rocks soothed her tortured soul. When she was restless or upset, these graves were where she'd return to, time after time. Here, she'd visit her brothers and listen to the calming noises of the river below.

A cold hurt gripped her heart today. She'd never be one of the sons her pa so wanted, dreamed of and lost. She'd never be the perfect cook and seamstress her ma hoped and still trained her to be. She was nothing more than Chancy Mallory. The maverick daughter who rode astride her favorite horse, could shoot with the best of the ranch hands, and could say a few unsavory words when the situation was appropriate and her parents weren't within earshot.

Bowie, her trusted mare, gave a snort of impatience behind her. Soon it would be suppertime, and if she didn't get back to the ranch house before long, her mother would have an extra twenty heinous ladylike chores for her to complete before she'd be allowed near the barn again.

"Goodbye," she whispered over her shoulder at the graves. She tucked the carved horse into her coat pocket and gathered Bowie's reins in her hand. In one fluid motion, she pulled herself into the saddle. Deftly, she rearranged her divided skirts to cover her legs. If she had it her way, she'd still wear men's trousers to ride in, but ma now forbid such unladylike behavior.

"Young lady, you'll wear a dress and act as a proper lady should. Your days of traipsing around like a boy need to come to an end." Those words chilled her heart. *I don't want to be a proper young lady. I want to ride the range chasing cattle, helping pa fix fences, and breaking the new colts each spring.*

With a heavy sigh, she nudged Bowie with her heels. They started the trek down the patchy snow-covered trail that lead to the ranch. The grave sites had been placed within easy walking distance for her ma, so she could come and visit her babes without much trouble, any time of year.

Chancy noticed the barn was busy with cowboys upon her return. The distinct sound of men's voices, spurs clanking with each step, and snorts of tired horses, filled her ears. A cowboy always cared for his horse before himself. A rule her father strictly enforced with the ranch hands.

The men were quick to do their chores and head for the dining hall with the smell of fresh baked bread and chili wafting in the air. Her ma prepared all the meals each day for the lot of them, a job Chancy knew her mother hoped to include her in. The thought of bustling around a kitchen brought a pout to her lips. *Not my idea of a good time.*

The last meal her mother had her prepare for the hands had been burnt to a crisp. *Who burns beans anyhow?* And her biscuits, one of the men had threatened to hit another upside the head and knock him out with the hardened lump. Chancy still bristled at the sniggers she'd heard at her expense.

She'd stepped into the room of hungry cowboys and glared them all down, hands planted firm against her hips. They'd been quick to apologize with her mother standing behind her. No one dared to complain since.

Chancy loosened the cinch at Bowie's side. She hefted the saddle off the horse and placed it on a rack nailed to the wall next to the horse's stall. She caught a glimpse of her father in the distance, talking with several of the ranch hands.

One, she realized she'd never seen before. His cowboy hat was pulled low and his getup, she noticed was well-worn, but clean and tidy. The other cowboys who had rode in off the range were covered in a thick layer of mud from the recent rains they'd had. Curious, she couldn't help but stare at the boy. Her father met her gaze across the distance with his deep sky-blue eyes and gave her a nod, before returning his attention back to the men.

Her father, Jim Mallory, was a intimidating figure to those around him. He was taller than most men, with wide muscular shoulders from years of hard work on the ranch. His faded chaps were tied about slim hips, and his hat was pushed back to expose bushy eyebrows. Chancy could tell he was deep in thought by the crinkles etched around his eyes. He twirled his salt and pepper mustache between his fingers.

Chancy decided to move closer to see what all the commotion was about. Her father's face, which was normally impassive, now held a thoughtful expression while he listened to the new hand talk. "I'm glad that you believe in starting colts with a firm, but gentle hand, Nick. We don't condone abuse of horses on this ranch," her father stated matter of fact, clapping the boy on the back in a friendly gesture. "I've been looking for a man who's good with horses for some time. They're hard to come by these days." Chancy noted his eyes held a hint of sadness.

"I always hoped one of my sons would carry on the Mallory ideals for training, but they left this earth too soon."

"Sorry to hear that, sir," the boy, whose name she gathered from the conversation was Nick, stated.

"Hi, Pa," Chancy interrupted.

A stab of jealousy struck her from out of nowhere. Jim was a man of few words, and praise was earned only when one demonstrated to him competence and good work ethic. She ground her teeth. The way her pa spoke to this boy like a long-lost friend rubbed her the wrong way. What's so special about this boy? she wondered.

Her father was a quiet, passionate man who wanted to build his ranch for future generations of Mallorys. Only all his sons had died before the age of ten. That left Chancy to carry on the family legacy. If she could convince her father to let her. As of late, he'd begun to agree with her mother that she needed to tend to her studies and pursue more womanly pursuits inside the house. The thought made her cringe.

"Chancy, shouldn't you be at the house by now?" her father asked.

She swallowed to hide the hurt from her voice."I was just headed that way. I need to check on Bowie one last time." She turned and sulked away. "He'll never understand," she muttered under her breath to no one in particular.

She took a deep, cleansing breath when she reached her horse. "I don't know what I'd do if I couldn't come and ride you every day." She hugged Bowie's neck tight. The horse's soft muzzle bumped against her coat pocket several times. "Don't worry, girl. I've got your treat right here." She reached into her coat pocket and pulled out a carrot. The horse took the treat from her open palm and crunched with an exaggerated content only a horse could show.

"Time for supper my friend." Chancy untied the lead from the stall door and led the mare inside. Earlier, she'd filled the horse's bin with fresh hay and grain. Bowie eagerly left her behind to make her way to the sweet grass that served as her evening meal.

Still deep in thought over the new ranch hand who followed her father about the barn, the sound of Deacon's gravelly voice, the ranch foreman, startled her. "Chancy, have you been riding out by Wild Horse Lake?"

The question caught her off guard, and her breath caught in her chest. She had indeed been at the lake as of late, but hoped no one would be the wiser. She'd been following the wild horse band, her eye on one of the colts. She'd told no one of her plan. Except her friend, Anna.

Anna was Deacon's daughter and her only girl friend. *She must have spilled the beans.* Lately, their friendship had changed. Anna, who once was her partner in adventure, now spent her time prattling on about boys and dresses. From her long, shiny black hair, to her large brown eyes and perfectly shaped lips, all the boys seemed to notice her now. Needless to say, Chancy had been avoiding her. She didn't care who Anna's latest love conquest at the ranch had been.

"Chancy?" the old man asked again.

"Yes, I was out there several days ago. Bowie needed a good run." She ducked her head, so Deacon couldn't read her expression.

"Well, keep your eyes open, the mustangs have been lingering close. You don't need one of those wild stallions challenging your horse."

"Don't worry, Deacon. I'll keep an eye out." Chancy glanced into the man's weathered face. He wasn't much taller than her these days. His once tall frame now was stooped with age, his legs bowed below the knees. He walked with a noticeable limp from an old leg injury, and this past winter, in the mornings his face would be scrunched with pain. This, he was always quick to hide behind a stern mask.

His deep brown eyes, a shade lighter than Anna's pierced into hers, gauging her response. She glanced to the ground, biting her cheek. *He doesn't quite believe me.* Without waiting another moment, Chancy ran out of the entrance of the barn and toward the main ranch house to eat her meal with her parents.

CHAPTER TWO

Chancy knew she was late by the frown on her mother's face when she opened the front door.

As fast as she could without making a mess of the fresh swept floor, she washed her face and hands in the basin her mother had left out in the front hall for such purposes. Refreshed and clean, Chancy stepped into the dining room.

"Chancy, I'd like you to meet our new ranch hand, Nick Stone."

The familiar tang of jealousy nipped at her heart with the mention of this name. Chancy's gaze went to her father's irritated one to that of the newcomer. Nick Stone met her direct stare from across the distance of the room. She brushed a stray hair from her face with annoyance. In the soft light of the dining room, Nick Stone watched her every move. A flush trailed up her neck and heated her cheeks to irritate her all the more.

"Your manners, please!" Chancy's mother, Alma, spoke in a low, cross tone.

"Sorry, ma...pa," she stammered.

"Nice to meet you, Nick." Chancy smiled as polite as she could muster and pulled out the chair next to her father. *I wish Nick Stone would disappear right now.* She plopped down on the chair, then quickly straightened before her mother reprimanded her and gave their guest a tight smile. Both her parents looked at her with vexed expressions.

"That's a nice mare you were riding earlier. What breed is she?" Nick asked from across the table.

Chancy looked into his eyes. They were the deepest blue she'd ever seen. For a moment, she'd been lost in their depths. A smile had crept onto Nick's face as he stared at her expectantly to answer.

Once again, the heat rushed to her cheeks.

"Bowie's a mustang," she managed to answer a moment later, without sounding too cross. Chancy glanced away and noticed her empty plate. Thankful to have something to do other than stare at her father's new ranch hand, she reached for the platter of chicken in front of her. She stabbed a hind leg and lifted the piece onto her plate, then passed the meat to her father.

"Mustangs are good mounts. I hope to capture a few for myself this summer. With your father's permission of course."

Taken aback by his answer, she glanced up once more. *No, I can't have him getting to the colt before I have a chance at him.*

"Deacon will help you pick out a string of horses for your use on the ranch tomorrow. We'll be rounding up the horses we keep in the valleys over the winter in a few weeks. There will be lots of colts needing worked. As for the mustangs, I allow each man to ride out and pick a fresh colt from the band, once a year. Bowie was captured several years ago and has been one of the best ranch horses we own."

Jim's voice took over the conversation, much to Chancy's relief. This gave her a moment to gather her thoughts and study Nick out of the corner of her eye. While her father and Nick talked ranch work and horseflesh, she concentrated on examining him.

Nick Stone had sandy blond hair cropped short about his ears and covering his forehead. His nose was long and straight, above a wide mouth which was quick to form an easy grin. His jawline was covered in a smattering of stubble. The feature which held her most captivated was his eyes. They were the bluest she'd ever seen. The color of the sky on a cloudless summer day. The type of day she'd sneak away with Bowie and lay hidden in the summer grasses while she dreamed of the future. She glanced away perplexed. Why Nick bothered her, she couldn't say.

When there was a lull in the ranch talk, Chancy decided to go out on a limb and ask a few questions of her own. "How old are you?" she blurted with more enthusiasm than she'd meant. She quickly took another bite of mashed potatoes to hide her interest.

"I turned eighteen a couple months ago," he replied.

His carefree answer irked her more. She was feeling snippier than a cinchy mare.

"Where are you from?"

This question seemed to bring him up short. Chancy glanced up from her plate. She'd hit a nerve. His expression was pained, and he stared into his plate, eyelashes lowered. He didn't answer immediately, instead he pushed some corn around his plate with his fork.

After several moments he cleared his throat. "My family's from back east. I struck out on my own more than a year ago and have worked my way west on several large ranches. Most recent one was in Nevada."

A vague answer at best, but piqued Chancy's curiosity, nonetheless. Just before she could get another question out, her mother stepped in.

"About your family, do you keep in touch?" Alma asked, her face awash in worry.

"Not much, ma'am. I sent them a letter some months back telling them I was headed toward Oregon."

His answer made her mother shudder. Alma's flawless skin paled as her dark eyes searched out her fathers. Chancy could see the hurt and loss which never seemed to leave her mother's gaze. One hand now rested above her heart while the other ran through her chestnut hair in a bun at the nap of her neck.

"Your mother must be heartbroken, Nick. While you're here, you should send her another note. At least let her know you're still alive and well. I could help you if you like?"

"Thank you, ma'am. I do know how to read and write though. I'll take your advice and send them another letter. I should have sooner, but wasn't sure where my travels would take me," Nick replied.

"Very well." Alma smoothed the front of her dress with her hand. "Chancy, please come and help in the kitchen."

"But, ma..."

"Chancy, do as your mother asks." Her father's annoyed tone left no room for argument.

Chancy clamped her lips tight and stood, "Nice to have met you, Nick." She studied him a moment before following her mother into the kitchen.

"How terrible," her mother commented as she shoved her hands into the sink full of soapy water. "That poor boy's mother..." Alma let out a long sigh.

With a sigh of her own, Chancy picked up the paring knife from the counter in one hand and a potato in the other. With long, brisk strokes she peeled the vegetable for the next day's breakfast. A little nag of never ending frustration struck her when she thought of the burdens her mother handled each day. Burdens she too would someday carry.

The continuous housework: cooking, cleaning, laundry. The garden which needed care daily, and on occasion being called to duty as a nurse to sick cows or horses, or worse case scenario, sick or injured men. The work took a toll on one's soul. Chancy could see the effects on Alma, her pale features and the dark shadows under her eyes that never went away.

Deacons's wife, Hilary, was her ma's constant companion at the house. The petite older woman with pale green eyes and thick silver hair she braided and wore wrapped around her head, visited daily.

The woman's help, along with her daughter and Chancy's friend, Anna, made the grind of each day tolerable, Chancy was sure. They were the only women on the ranch. The majority of the men who were ranch hands on the Mallory ranch were single and drifters. Much like Nick.

Nick. Her thoughts returned to his features. She supposed he was considered handsome by other girls her age. She wouldn't be surprised if her friend Anna hadn't used her charms on him already.

Every other cowboy on the place seemed enchanted by her. *Why should I care?* If only every time his name crossed her mind her body didn't heat up warmer than the noonday sun. This sensation had never occurred around the other ranch hands her father had hired in the past; in fact this had never happened before at all.

Other than when I see a particular horse I like, such as the rare mustang colt she'd followed these last months. That—made her flush and her heart would race with excitement. She would make the colt her own this spring.

"Chancy, take your father and Nick a cup of coffee and a couple slices of that pie on the counter."

Thoughts interrupted, Chancy glanced up. "Yes, ma."

Chancy left the peeled potatoes on the table and did her mother's bidding. With two cups of steaming coffee in her hand, she returned to the dining room with a smile.

"Chancy, Nick is going to take over your chores in the barn. This will give you more time at the house with your mother to help her and work on your lessons.

"What!" Her heart dropped to her stomach. Chancy's hands trembled and coffee spilled about her feet. Her mind went into a tailspin. *No, no, no...* "But, Pa, I can handle my chores at the barn and help ma in the house. Please, I enjoy helping outside." Chancy cringed at the pleading tone in her voice, but she couldn't help it.

"I don't mind at all, Chancy. I'll make sure Bowie is well taken care of for you." Nick's tone was meant to comfort, but Chancy's hackles raised anyhow.

"Chancy, you're sixteen. It's time you start acting like a lady. I won't have my daughter riding among men: spitting, chewing and cussing."

"I don't do any of those things and you know it." She straightened her shoulders in a struggle to keep her composure. "I'm a good shot, I can wrangle a horse as good as any of those cowboys, and I'm a hard worker." She raised her chin.

"I didn't say you didn't work hard. What I want is for you

to learn to work hard inside the house.

These are lessons every young woman must learn. Your mother told me even Anna has moved onto more womanly endeavors helping with the household chores. You can too. You can still return to the barn in the evenings for a ride on Bowie."

Chancy didn't know whether she wanted to scream or cry. She clamped her lips tight, to avoid saying something she'd regret as her pa's attention returned to Nick Stone. *Nick Stone, I wish you'd never came here,* she fumed. With his presence on this ranch, he'd managed to change the course of her life in one evening. This didn't sit well in her craw.

CHAPTER THREE

Nick watched intently as Chancy strode out of the ranch house, the door slamming behind her as she followed the path toward the barn at a brisk walk. For the last several days, he'd noticed her daily routine was the same. Each afternoon, when her house chores were complete, she'd rush out the door. Once outside, she'd take a look around, and if no adults were in the vicinity, she'd run to the barn.

He turned to walk back inside, hanging a bridle he'd been cleaning on a hook protruding from the wall. Chancy entered the barn, her duster flapped about her boot heels, and a hat covered her long auburn hair which she wore in a braid down her back. Nick looked away. He shouldn't be watching the ranch owner's daughter, no matter how pretty she might be. And feisty.

"Hi," Nick called as Chancy stomped by. He caught the flash of her brown eyes, brimming with suspicion. He recalled dinner the night before. She'd watched him warily throughout the meal, her eyes full of spark each time he caught her gaze. From what little he knew of her, he could tell she had spirit.

Her direct personality reminded him of his sister, Elsie. A little spitfire.

"I took good care of Bowie today. Even brushed out her mane and tail for you," he offered.

"You don't have to do that. She's my horse—my responsibility."

Nick flinched at the snap in her voice. With a shrug, he left her to go about his chores, not wanting to stir the hornets nest further. With a glance in her direction every so often, he couldn't help but notice her struggle with something over the saddle next to Bowie's stall. Curious what prolonged her ride, he decided to walk over and offer a hand.

"Can you use some help?" he asked in a light-hearted tone. He peered over her shoulder. Being so close to her, he noticed the few freckles spaced strategically over her pert nose. Her lips, which formed a thin line, never cracked a smile, but were lush for a kiss... *Stop.*

He was shocked by his reaction to her. He had to draw the line right there. If his thoughts continued in this direction, there'd be nothing but trouble for him. She was attempting to mend a ripped stirrup leather on her saddle. She struggled to tighten the leather ties which were laced through a ring attached to the saddle and held the stirrup leather in place. It was in his nature to want to help, but when she turned her head and glared at him, he decided it best to back away.

"No, I'm fine," she answered with finality.

He decided to walk away, let her fight her own battles. He didn't know her well enough, and from what he did know she was more bristly than a cornered porcupine. He grabbed a shovel and rake which were propped against the wall and headed for the farthest stall from her. Out of her sight and out of her path. At least this way he couldn't irritate her further.

Chancy bristled as Nick disappeared from view. She'd rushed out of the house for a ride this afternoon, only to find her saddle had a ripped stirrup leather. Dang. If she didn't fix the saddle now, she'd risk her safety if there was an emergency out in the wild. If the leather ripped at an inopportune time, she could be dislodged from the horse, hurt, or even killed. Her father, if he found out she hadn't taken the time to properly care for her tack, would never let her return to the barn again.

When Nick had looked over her shoulder, his breath warm against her neck, it had almost been her undoing. Her heart still pounded against her ribcage, and her body tingled throughout just with the thought. These were sensations she'd never experienced before, and they both thrilled and scared her. It was better not to worry about these feelings now. She'd store them away for further contemplation, when she had time to ponder such emotions.

"Good enough," she mumbled under her breath. The saddle was fixed, but the chore had taken time out of her afternoon ride. She'd have to ride hard to reach the area she sought today. Without another glance in Nick's direction, she led Bowie out of her stall. True to his word, Nick had brushed out her dark mane and tail which was interlaced with strands of silver. In the ray of light which filtered through the entrance, her mare's dun hide gleamed with golden perfection. She should have been thankful for the kind deed, but instead the gesture seemed to eat away at her patience.

Was he always this nice? Her father adored their new hand. Every night this past week all he had spoken about at the supper table was Nick said this, or Nick did that. Same with her friend, Anna.

She'd talked until she was blue in the face over how wonderful the new ranch hand was.

Nick was especially good with horses, she'd learned through her parents' conversation. "Picked the best horses from the corral. That boy knows his horse flesh." Pride shown bright in her pa's voice.

The boy was a saint in her father's eyes. Why do I care, she wondered? The answer was always the same in her mind. *Because I'll never be one of the sons, my father desired.*

Chancy checked the cinch on her saddle one last time before she put her boot in the stirrup and swung her leg over Bowie's hindquarter. Her gaze met Nick's across the distance. He leaned against a shovel and shoved his cowboy hat above his forehead. His blue eyes seemed to narrow in on her every move. Heat permeated her cheeks with the realization. Chancy glanced away and gathered Bowie's reins in her hand. She remembered to smooth her skirts over her legs to protect them from the cold and not "compromise her femininity," in her mother's words.

She cast one last guarded look in Nick's direction. He reached for his hat and tipped the edge.

Chancy ignored the gesture and instead dug her heels into Bowie's sides. The horse lunged forward at a gallop. When out of sight of the barn, she pulled Bowie into a brisk trot. The air was crisp, Chancy could see each breath the horse took before her. The air numbed her face, but the chill brought her senses alive and she felt free. Free as the rugged lands before her.

The filtered spring afternoon sun glimmered off the delicate, frozen purple petals of numerous wildflowers. They grew sporadic between the bunches of sagebrush and sparse junipers spread across the land. Spring in the Steens was a wonderful time of year.

The earth smelled fresh and new. Quail, pheasants, and all the other birds in the area chirped and hunted with contentment. Best of all were the wild horses, returned to feed and roam through the area. Each year the herd grew larger with strong new colts. Bowie was born of this herd, and the best horse on the ranch. Her pa said so many times.

Chancy pulled Bowie to a halt. A slight breeze tickled her neck and rustled the bunchgrass and sagebrush at her heels. She listened for signs the herd may be near. A faint whinny could be heard in the distance. *Yes,* her heart pounded. Her pulse raced with excitement. The colt she'd been watching, she hoped, would show himself today. The colt she was determined to capture.

In her mind, she'd already named the fleet of foot mustang. Snowbar seemed a fitting name for the white leopard colt with a silver mane and tail. He was different from the rest of the herd. As she'd heard her father say, he was likely a throwback from a mare which escaped capture after the surrender of the great Chief Joseph years earlier. Another melancholy story told from her father's point of view.

"The cavalry confiscated the tribe's horses after they surrendered. The best of the Appaloosa's that didn't manage to escape into the wilderness were sold. Those that didn't sell, the men shot."

The thought of someone wanting to kill these beautiful creatures was beyond Chancy's comprehension. Lost in thought, she hadn't noticed the group of horses in the distance. Bowie snorted, ears pricked forward on alert.

Chancy squeezed her legs into Bowie's sides and the horse moved out. The closer she came, the more horses she recognized from the year before. Many of the mares watched with a protective eye over the new foals at their sides. The spindly legged miniatures, frolicked and played. A nip at one's backside earned another a hoof in the chest. Rough play for when they grew into adult horses and needed to survive these harsh lands. The sight brought a smile to Chancy's lips.

Her breath caught in her chest with the appearance of the colt. Her colt. *Snowbar...* He galloped across the meadow, tail pointed toward the sky, mane flowing against his neck and shoulder. A sight to behold. He'd grown this past year. He would be a little over two years old now. Old enough for her to capture and make into the best horse ever.

Chancy realized her error with a start when the stallion let out a scream of warning. She'd wandered too close to the herd. A chill creeped down her spine and she glanced around. Bowie snorted and pawed at the ground, muscles bunched and ready to buck. "Easy, girl." She patted the mare's side to calm her.

"Chancy, what the hell do you think you're doing?" Her father's words rang out from behind her.

She turned, jumping out of her skin as her father and Deacon pull their horses to a halt behind her. Her father's lips held a firm line, his eyebrows knit into a deep frown. Deacon held a similar expression.

"Where's your rifle, Chancy? Haven't I told you enough times never to ride out on the range without your rifle? There are bears, cougars, rouge stallions..." He pointed to the agitated stallion in the distance, "that would love to tear you to shreds. Where's your head, girl?"

Chancy's heart dropped. *How could I have been so irresponsible? If only I hadn't been so intent on getting away from Nick earlier.* She clenched her jaw tight. Reaching down, sure enough her scabbard was missing. In fact, she was so focused on leaving for her ride, the thought of if her rifle was attached to the saddle hadn't even crossed her mind.

"Sorry, Pa," she managed to say. There really was no excuse.

"Ride on back to the ranch. There's a spring storm in the making, and I don't want you caught out in it."

Sure enough, incoming ominous black clouds were fast approaching. This time of year it wasn't uncommon for a spring storm to blow in and coat the earth in fresh layers of snow. With one last glance at Snowbar, who now grazed in the distance, Chancy turned Bowie around and loped for home.

CHAPTER FOUR

Nick wiped a bead of perspiration from his brow. The colt he worked in the corral was covered in a fine sheen of sweat, but had begun to relax and follow his cues. He stood directly in the center of the corral, with only a rope in his hand.

With his gaze locked into the colt's, he took a quick, aggressive step forward. The horse fled to the farthest corner. A horse's nature was to fight or take flight. Nick waved his arms in the air, and the colt raced around the enclosure in a nervous frenzy. Nick held direct eye contact with the fleeing colt.

His shoulders and body remained straight and rigid to provoke the colt to remain in a forward motion. Around and around the horse went. Nick wondered about this colt. The horse continued his flight, refusing to yield.

Then, within the span of a heartbeat, the magic began. The young horse relaxed, and his head dropped low. The colt used his ears to follow and listen for Nick's next movement. The colt licked his lips, head still lowered.

The sign of submission; excitement built in Nick's gut with this small success. Next, Nick dropped his eye contact and took a step back. The colt slowed his pace, ears still pointed toward him, gauging his every move. The colt was now at a trot and snorted from his exertion.

Nick turned his back on the colt, the final part of the process. He stood stock still, waiting for the colt's response. When he lifted his gaze, he saw Chancy standing beside her father and several of the other hands. Jim smiled at him, a look of approval shining in his eyes. The hands, Slim and Chet, clapped their hands.

"Sure some fancy work you did there," Chet called out.

Nick nodded in their direction before casting a glance

toward Chancy. He should have looked away, but he was locked into her deep brown eyes, which were wide with fascination. The idea that he'd surprised her somehow made his heart skip a beat faster.

Nick felt a soft bump against his shoulder. Then another. He turned, slow and steady, then reached up and gave the horse a pat between his soft brown eyes. The horse dropped his head and allowed Nick to run his hands down his sleek gray neck, across his back and down his legs.

"That's a great technique you have there, son," Mr. Mallory stated."I haven't seen one of those broomtails soften toward a human since Chancy worked with Bowie. Keep up the good work."

"Thank you kindly, sir." Nick beamed with the compliment.

"We have a few rough horses that could use some of that magic. I'll have the men bring them in off the range tomorrow for Nick to take a crack at," Deacon said, as he joined the group.

"Sounds reasonable," Jim agreed, gazing at Nick. "You up for the challenge, Nick?"

"Yes, sir. I'll give them a try."

"Well then, we'll see you in the morning." The men then stepped away from the fence and walked toward the main house. Chet and Slim returned to the barn. Nick's gaze returned to Chancy.

Her lips were pinched, and her eyes narrowed at him. In fact, she wore the same irritated expression his mother used to have when he or his brother Jed or sister Elise had done something mischievous. The thought of his mother brought a tinge of homesickness and guilt to his heart. He hadn't thought of his family in weeks now. He'd been so immersed in ranch life at the Mallory's, that thoughts of home had been pushed into the deepest recesses of his mind.

Nick's mother, he suspected, would be pining over his absence. He'd left home a little over a year ago now with only a note left on his pillow in his bedroom. He hadn't sent but one letter since, some months ago, telling his parents he was alive and well and headed further west.

His father, he was sure, hadn't skipped a beat with his departure. Matthew Stone, a prominent banker in Boston, was a man devoid of emotion. He provided for his family, and did this well, but when it came to emotions... caring, love, affection, were not words that existed in his vocabulary.

Hard work, success, prominence were what the man lived for and wanted for his sons. This was one of the reasons Nick had left home to strike out on his own. His father had internships scheduled for his brother Jed and himself when they came of age. Jed had been with the bank two years, and this year Nick also would have started at the bank. If he hadn't left home.

"That's some fancy process you have there."

Chancy's words broke him from his memories. Her brown eyes glittered with icicles. She swiped a lock of wispy hair from her eyes, her face scrunched as she looked him over warily.

"Thanks," he responded, not knowing what else to say. Instead, he walked away. As he made his way west, he'd been taught this colt training process by an old Indian on one of the many ranches he'd worked at. The old man, whose name was Talking Bear, pulled him aside one day after Nick had been put in charge of caring for the ranch hands' horses.

There was a maverick mare none of the other cowboys would touch. They kept her in a pen away from the other horses. It was said by the cowboys, she was meaner than a cornered she-bear.

She'd bite and kick at anyone or any horse who dared to come near her. The ranch owner didn't want her put down because of her beauty. She was a golden palomino with a silver mane and tail. She had the sought after confirmation of a working cow pony, so many of the cowboys wanted in a horse.

"Boy, take that horse into the corral and follow my instruction. When you're done, that little mare will be eating out of your hand. Those other pigheaded, so called cowboys, haven't looked past the outer core of this special horse. In you, I see a gentle soul whose spirit is one with horses."

"How do you know that?" Nick asked. The words the grizzled old man spoke had intrigued him.

He'd always held a fascination for horses. One of the reasons he'd left home. Not locked away in some stuffy old office; full of dust, cognac, and rich mahogany furniture, which his father seemed to prefer.

"Follow my instructions, young man, for I see the magic inside you."

With a chill down his spine at the old man's words, he'd done his bidding. Getting the wild eyed mare out of her pen and into the corral had nearly cost him his life. He'd never forget those sharp hooves as they'd flashed before his face. But he'd managed after a bit to get her cooperation. Then, with step-by-step instruction from the old Indian, he lay his hands on the horse's beautiful hide that day.

Every day for two weeks when all the other ranch hands were at work, Talking Bear and he would bring out the mare and work her in the corral. By the second week, he was on her back. She was a fast and eager learner, and Nick had never been so proud.

"You have the magic, boy. Don't ever let anyone take that from you," Talking Bear told him later that evening, when the others had retired to their bunks. Talking Bear would sit on the porch, under a blanket of stars and smoke his pipe each evening. His long white braids lay against his chest, and his face, rough as leather, was always deep in concentration.

Nick took those words to heart. He'd left the ranch soon after. It was one place he would never return. One of the ranch hands had taken the mare from her stall when he'd been out checking fence-line. It was said he'd prodded her with his sharp California style spurs and she gave him a fight. The mare threw him off time after time, and in a fit of anger, he'd tied her to the pole in the middle of the corral. He then beat her with a whip. The harder she fought, the more lashes he gave her until, finally, she strangled herself in a slow and painful death.

Nick found her, still lying in the dirt and dust, covered in bloody welts from the whip and gouges in her sides from the spurs. He'd never witnessed such malicious cruelty in his life. Never had he been so angry with a person before. He just about gave up his dream and returned home because of it. Only, at this point, he didn't know where home was.

Heartbroken and sick, Nick packed his meager belongings and left the ranch the same day. He'd drifted from place to place until now. The Mallory Ranch had a good reputation. Mr. Mallory was known as a kind and fair man. He didn't believe in abuse of animals, and his ranch hands were required to share the philosophy. Any man caught mistreating a horse, or any other animal on the property would be fired immediately.

Nick, finished with his work with the colt, pulled himself over the top rail of the corral. Chancy had disappeared into the barn, to check on Bowie, he was sure. He'd heard she'd been grounded to the house after riding out on the range without her rifle for protection. Nick watched her return to the barn, afternoon after afternoon, but she never left for a ride. He never bothered her, but left her in peace to visit with her horse.

Chancy sighed and rested her head on her arms crossed in front of her on the rail of Bowie's stall. She pulled the wooden horse out of her pocket. The relic was smooth from years of handling. The horse was running, and Chancy liked to imagine it was a mustang. She turned it over and over in her palm. Though a toy she was much too old for, the familiar weight of the horse in her hand calmed her.

The mare nudged her with a warm nose, her ears pricked forward, eyes alight with question about her young mistress. Chancy blew softly into the horse's nostrils and the mare let out a sigh of her own before sneezing. This brought laughter to Chancy's lips.

"Oh, Bowie, I can't wait until I can take you out on a ride again."

The last few weeks had been tedious. From sun up to

sun down she'd been stuck indoors. She missed the afternoon breeze, the smell of horses, sweat, and leather when the cowboys returned to the ranch each afternoon. The easy laughter and joking of the hands while they cared for their horses.

In the house this past week, to her great horror, she'd overheard a conversation between her parents. "I think it would be wonderful for Chancy to experience the culture of the city. I've wanted to visit with Bethany for some time. It's been years since we've seen each other."

Chancy's mind went numb with her mother's words. She'd left the room, heart pounding, stomach in a knot with the thought. Ranch life was busy. She must have misunderstood. Her parents wouldn't plan to send a needed, capable, working hand away from the ranch. Calmer, she moved the conversation to the back of her mind.

Chancy continued to help her mother all week in the house. Her ma told her she wished to use this time to improve her cooking and sewing skills. Chancy had tried her darndest to please her mother, she swore she did, but the frequent looks of frustration aimed in her direction told her she was still lacking in domestic skills.

She hadn't meant to add so much salt to the eggs at breakfast a few mornings ago. It was just that she'd glanced out the window and watched the horses as they frolicked in the corral. The cool spring mornings and new green grass full of sugars made them rambunctious as they bucked and snorted around the enclosure.

Then, there was her friend Anna to contend with. She was a natural in the kitchen, much to Chancy's chagrin. Anna's pancakes turned out so fluffy this morning. She was unable to compete with her friend's skills in front of the stove. Her mother and Hilary had praised her with delight while Chancy hung in the shadows.

Then, today after lunch, she'd poked a needle through some material meant for a dress straight into her finger. The wound had bled on her mother's fancy lace she'd purchased at their last visit in town. She still cringed at the dark look her mother had given her over this mishap.

"Will I ever be the ladylike daughter my mother desires? Why can't pa just let me work outside?
That's where I was meant to be. I just know it. Riding fence line in the dead of winter doesn't bother me none. Neither does branding, or castrating the calves. That's my favorite time of year. Not even the books pa keeps in his office scare me. Those numbers show how much hard work everyone has put into making the Mallory Ranch a success."

"It's nice knowing someone likes those dreaded books."

It was her father's voice. She turned, her pa stood behind her, a hint of amusement danced in his blue eyes.

"Your mother tells me you've worked hard all week and put effort into learning the more domestic side of ranching. I appreciate you taking your grounding and making good use of your time. You have my permission to ride again as long as a few rules are followed.

The first being you will always carry your rifle with you when out riding on the range. The second is your mother and I would like for one of the ranch hands to ride with you, if they are available. I don't like the thought of you out there on your own. Deal?"

"Yes—thank you, Pa!" Chancy dove into his arms. Her heart beat with excitement. Her weeks of purgatory were over, and the colt was within her reach once more.

CHAPTER FIVE

The table was alight with lively conversation the next morning. "I'm expecting this year will be prosperous with plenty of good colts to round up for the big sale up north. And cattle prices are at an all-time high. With lots of hard work, I think the Mallory Ranch should break even, and maybe have a little extra to boot this year."

"Oh, Jim, that's wonderful news. We are blessed with the hands we've acquired these past years. Having good help makes all the difference." Alma's face was flushed with enjoyment.

"I agree with you there, Alma, and since we've found and hired on Nick Stone...I must admit, that boy has a good head on his shoulders. He knows his horseflesh and isn't afraid to get his hands dirty. Next to Deacon, I'd say he's my best man."

Chancy heard Nick's name and bristled. She tried to not be jealous of the boy. He was everything her pa said and more. He'd given her more tips on how to work with Bowie and improve their communication this last week...but the praise her father gave him still rankled her.

"Nick has himself quite the string of horses now. Like I said a while back, he picked the best out of the bunch. With his gentle hand, he's got a string of good cow ponies in the works." Her father's voice was filled with pride.

"I've been thinking, Alma, with Nick's mind for horses—if we do get a little ahead, I'd like to purchase a good breeding stock stud for the ranch. How would you feel about adding in some good horseflesh to the Mallory Ranch Legacy?"

"Oh, Jim, I think that would be wonderful. If you think you can make it happen, do it."

Chancy noted the dreamy state in her mother's eyes. She recalled that had always been a dream of her fathers, to have the best working cow horses in the west. She'd overheard him speak of this with Deacon on numerous occasions.

"Sounds wonderful, Pa," Chancy added."But haven't you noticed the colts in the mustang band this year? The leopard colt?" Her heart froze while she waited for his answer.

"Those are some nice colts, but they're nothing but mustangs, Chancy. Folks around these parts are looking for purebred ranch horses. That's where the future of the Mallory Ranch will be."

Her father's words stung to the core. Mustangs were and always would be range bred broomtails in her father's eyes. But the leopard colt was something special. He had grace and a magical aura about him. Chancy was going to make him hers, and soon.

"May I be excused?" Chancy set her cloth napkin on the table.

"Yes, dear. I suppose we should get started about the day." Alma pushed her chair back from the table and reached for her empty plate.

"Chancy, can you help with the dishes? I'm going to get started on the desert pies for the men."

"Sure, Ma." Chancy gathered as many of the dishes as she could carry in her arms, then walked into the kitchen. Her pa continued to sit at the table, a mug of coffee in one hand and stroking his mustache with the other deep in thought, she suspected on the future plans of the Mallory Ranch.

***

Chancy watched as Anna made perfect stitches in the needle point she had near completion. A dreamy look overcame her olive features. "Oh, Chancy, that Nick Stone, he's such a gentleman. Did you know, he has the bluest eyes ever? I could gaze into them all day and never grow bored." Chancy looked away, so her friend wouldn't see her rolling her eyes.

Anna raised her fingers to her lips, a whimsical look on her features."I'm going to get him to kiss me, you just wait." A lovesick smile came over her lips. She cast a glance at Chancy and batted her eyelashes coyly. "Unless you call first dibs that is."

Chancy swallowed hard, so she wouldn't choke on her irritation. Anna had been her friend since childhood. She couldn't remember a day when Anna and her mother didn't come to the house, to either visit or work. She was like a sibling in all respects but blood to Chancy.

"No, I don't like Nick that way," she blurted out.

"Good, that's what I was hoping you'd say," Anna replied, victorious.

Chancy wondered about her words the rest of the day, after Anna left with her mother. If she didn't care that Anna wanted to chase after Nick like a love sick puppy, why did little jabs of anger keep her stomach knotted in turmoil all day. It made no sense. Instead of pondering it further, she pushed the thoughts to the back of her mind. She would worry about Nick and Anna later. Just like she'd worry about the conversation her parents had discussed of visiting back east. Better to not think of it until necessary. Right now she needed to stay focused on her plan. To capture Snowbar.

***

Later in the afternoon, after the house chores were complete, Chancy ran down the path toward the barn. Running wasn't considered ladylike, but her mother was busy with a baby quilt she was making for a neighbor. She wouldn't be looking out the window anytime soon.

It was pleasant outside, the sun warmed the earth and not a cloud was in the sky. A perfect day for a ride. She bounded inside the barn.

"What's the hurry?"

The sound of Nick's voice stopped her up short before she reached Bowie's stall. She turned, his deep blue eyes twinkled with curiosity. A friendly smile touched his lips as he joined her at the gate of her horse's stall.

"I'm riding out on the range. I want to try and catch up with the band of mustangs." She didn't want to tell him her full plans; to fix up the holding pen the cowboys used when they rounded the mustangs up each year. She planned to use the pen to capture the colt.

"Can I come with you? I'm done for the day and planned on riding one of my new colts today anyhow."

The idea of Nick riding with her set her on edge. Anna's words of earlier crossed her mind. But her father's words won out. He thought she needed a chaperone when she rode, when one was available. If he found out she'd refused Nick's offer, there could be more trouble ahead for her.

The problem was she'd sworn him as an enemy in her mind. Competition for her father's affections. But, it would be rude to say no. Especially when he looked so excited to join her.

"Okay," she replied after a long pause.

They saddled their horses in companionable silence. "Don't forget your rifle," Nick commented while he put his own in the scabbard attached to his saddle.

"I don't plan to," Chancy replied, clenching her jaw. "I've been riding this range for as long as I can remember. I can take care of myself," she grumbled.

"I never said you couldn't. Look, Chancy, I'm sorry. I meant no offense by what I said. I just don't want you to get in trouble with your pa again."

Chancy glanced in Nick's direction. His face appeared sincere. There was no hint of malice in his words. She brushed off the whole confrontation.

"Let's go." She swung herself into the saddle and fixed her skirts around her ankles while she waited for Nick to mount his colt. They trotted through the grassy meadows, the horses' hooves sucked to the ground on the still marshy surface as they rode toward the mountains. The wild horses, she figured wouldn't be far from where she'd last seen them. The grasses were lush this time of year and water abundant. They wouldn't stray far from either.

"Your pa says we'll be rounding up the band later this summer. He lets the men take their pick of which mustang they want. Are you planning on selecting a new horse?"

Nick's question caught her off guard. Should she tell him of Snowbar, and her plans for capturing and keeping the colt on her own? He would find out soon enough, fresh tracks on the ground made it clear the herd was near.

"Look!" Nick pointed in the distance. A white mare and foal grazed near a stream. Farther beyond them the mustangs basked in the afternoon sun. Some grazing, others in groups dusting the flies off one another with their tails.

"Snowbar..." Chancy murmured. The leopard colt pranced around the perimeter of the group, head held high, tail flowing in the wind.

She sensed Nick was watching her and cursed the heat rising to her cheeks. It was too late to hide her feelings now.

"Is that the horse you've picked?" Nick returned his gaze to Snowbar. "Those are the most unusual markings I've ever seen on a horse. Just look at him."

Chancy's heart skipped a beat with Nick's apparent awe of the horse. "I plan to make him mine."
Her voice little over a whisper.

Nick's head jerked in her direction, his eyebrow raised in question.

"He's mine," she repeated and kicked Bowie into a gallop toward the mustangs.

Chancy kept Bowie far enough from the mustangs so not to disturb them or irritate the stallion. Their leader was a stout bay. Her father said this stallion had a line of draft running in his veins which explained his thick body and large, wide feet. A white blaze drifted down his face. A long black mane full of tangles and brambles covered his neck. He kept his ears forward and alert, watching the approaching riders with eyes as direct as a hawk.

When Chancy was close enough, she pulled Bowie to a stop and watched Snowbar from the distance. The young colt remained on the outskirts of the band with a small group of his peers. If left in the wild, he and the others would be sent away by the stallion soon. They'd leave in search of their own future bands.

She heard Nick's horse behind her, but she didn't turn and look at him.

"So how do you plan on capturing this wild young colt on your own?"

Chancy didn't answer right away. This was something she'd been contemplating in her mind for weeks now. She chewed on her lower lip, deciding the best way to answer.

"I haven't quite figured that part out yet." She turned Bowie, so she faced Nick and the colt he rode. Nick sat relaxed in the saddle, arms crossed over his chest as he watched her. He didn't appear judgmental, and this softened her opinion of him.

"There's a rough built corral the hands use every year to run the mustangs into at the end of this valley. I was going to try and herd him in there myself. I just need to keep a wary eye on the stallion and make sure he doesn't attack me while I'm trying to pull it off."

"Take me to this enclosure. I'd like to get a good look at the rest of this stretch of land anyhow."

Chancy nodded. Her curiosity of Nick ate away at her. As they rode, she wanted to ask him about his life, his family, but she couldn't find the nerve. Didn't want to pry. Instead, they rode along the outskirts of the mustang herd in silence.

"My pa says Snowbar's a throwback," she said a few minutes later. "His lineage runs back to the horses the Nez Perce once bred. They were called the Palouse horse. Deacon called him an Appaloosa.

He's the only one my pa or even Deacon have seen in this area since before the Indians."

"I've never seen anything like him. He's a rare find for sure," Nick commented. "I've heard stories though about this type of horse. One of the ranches I worked at had an ole timer who liked to tell tall stories, so I thought. I guess he proved me wrong."

"What kind of stories?"

"Well, he was old, as I mentioned and had worked on ranches all over, from Mexico to Montana in his lifetime. At one of the larger more prestigious ranches he worked, they had a Chinese cook. 'Best damned food he'd ever ate,' he always said. "Anyway, the cook liked to tell stories of his country. When a stranger rode in one day on a black horse, black as night mind you, with white spotted hindquarters the little cook lit up like a firecracker. The Chinese man told the old timer that in China, these horses were considered enchanted. They were superior to all other horses and his kinsman sometimes called them 'heavenly horses.'"

Chancy held onto his every word. *Heavenly horses,* Snowbar certainly was heavenly. She had to agree with that.

"Unfortunately I can't remember any other details. At the time, I just thought he was a crazy old man telling stories. I didn't think there'd be any truth to his words. I guess that goes to prove you should never discount your elders."

"Thanks for sharing the story with me, Nick. I certainly believe it could be true."

Snowbar had a certain magnetism about him. Nick's story just proved legends could be true.

Chancy realized she was more relaxed in Nick's company the longer they rode together. She was eager for him to share a little more about his life.

"Where were you raised?" she asked, after a bit.

Nick took a long time to answer, a dark shadow fell over his face, his blue eyes became hooded.

I never should have intruded on his privacy, she chided herself.

"My family's from Boston." He finally answered.

"Do you have any brothers or sisters?" The question escaped her lips before she could stop herself.

"Yes, I've an older brother, Jed. He works with my father at the bank. Then, Elsie, is my younger sister. She's your age, I think? She just turned seventeen."

"I'm sixteen," Chancy answered.

"How about yourself, no other older brothers or sisters?" Nick asked.

His quick change of the subject made her wonder how much he must miss his family. A shadow of guilt crossed his features, but he disguised it with his sudden interest in her family.

"My brothers all died when they were young as you've probably heard. All three of them are laid to rest on the hill just past the house, overlooking the river. They contracted some kind of sickness, one after the other. Their deaths just about killed my parents. To lose all their boys at once. My brothers' were to carry on the Mallory family legacy."

"I'm sorry," Nick stated.

"That's why I have to capture this colt. To show my pa, just because I'm a girl, doesn't mean I can't work this land as well as any one of my brothers would have if they'd have lived." Chancy pulled her horse to a stop.

"Well this is it." They'd reached the end of the valley. Hidden in a grove of Junipers, a rough corral had been erected. The enclosure was built wide enough to stay out of reach of the wild horse's flashing hooves, but high enough and built strong enough to keep the horses contained.

"I think your plan might just work," Nick said. His gaze followed the length of the corral. It was built over a small stream, so the horses would have water. There was also abundant grass at the moment so feed wouldn't need to be brought in.

"What would you say if I offered to help you capture your colt? Would you give me a chance?"

Chancy was speechless. She stared at Nick and her heart did a flip-flop. *He would help me?*

Excitement built in the pit of her stomach. Her dream was within reach, and with Nick's help she'd be able to succeed.

"I'd love to have your help on one condition." She searched for any signs of disagreement.

"What's that?" Nick asked.

"You don't mention this to my father. I want Snowbar to

be a surprise."

Nick stunned her when he reached out his hand. "Deal."

"Deal." She returned his smile. His hand was rough and firm in her smaller one. The contact sent a jolt of something unknown through her bloodstream. She thought her heart might beat out of her chest with the extent of this new feeling.

Nick's hand dropped to his side. "We've got work to do."

CHAPTER SIX

Chancy awoke to another sun filled morning. She jumped out of bed and raced to the window as she did each morning. The barn and corral were in view from her bedroom. She'd stare down the path and watch the ranch hands gather their horses from the holding pens and saddle up for a day's work.

The sight of morning light across the backs of fresh horses, and cowboys with their dusters on, swinging a lariat to catch their favorite mount always exhilarated her and pride would well up in her heart.

After the day's work inside the house was complete, she'd be down there among them. Working with Nick. The thought made her heart start to flutter. She saw Nick in a new light since their truce.

Every afternoon she'd leave the confines of the house and watch Nick. He worked with the yearlings, started the colts under saddle, and even worked with a few rogue horses the other cowboys had since tossed to the side.

"That boy knows how to charm a horse and convince him it's his idea to take to the saddle. I've never seen anything like it." Her father's words echoed in her mind. The best part was, and her father didn't realize this, Nick was also teaching her everything he knew about his training techniques. The other cowboys guffawed, and called him lucky, but Chancy saw something brilliant in the way he worked each horse.

Her only worry was Anna. She was her best friend, and she noticed all the time Nick and she were together. She'd said words earlier which had shocked and pained her. "Chancy, you said you weren't interested in Nick, so why are you with him all the time? I'm not blind, you know."

Chancy had been taken aback with the vehemence in her

friend's words. *I don't like Nick in that way.* Or maybe I do? The last few days, she wondered if maybe Anna was on to something she just hadn't figured out yet.

"Ma, the kitchen's clean, I'm heading outside," Chancy called to her mother who crocheted as she rocked in her rocker in the front room.

"If your father's home and in the barn, tell him to come on up to the house. I have something I need to discuss with him."

"Sure Ma—will do." Her father was due back at any time. He and Deacon had traveled east to check on a stud her father hoped to add to the ranch stock. She hoped her father would be back, she wasn't allowed to ride out on the range in his absence. Not even with a chaperone. And the colt beckoned to her.

Chancy stepped onto the front porch and sat in a rocker. She pulled on her riding boots, then stood and straightened her skirts. With her mother near the window, she'd walk to the barn today. Only yesterday, her ma had commented on her tomboyish ways once again.

"Chancy, you're sixteen, soon you'll be thinking of marriage and children. The time for horses and riding and ranching should be left to the men. You should take after Anna more. She's become quite the seamstress. I think she misses you now, more than ever."

"Ma, I will never give up riding. It's in my blood," she'd argued. "And I spend every day with Anna. I can't help the fact she's a more accomplished cook and seamstress than me. She doesn't know how to hitch up the buggy or lasso one of the calves. Both things I'm quite proficient at."

Alma had let out a sigh with the comments, hands on her hips, she looked Chancy over with a befuddled expression.

"All in good time I expect." She'd left the room, dress swishing about her boots without further comment.

Fear had clutched at Chancy's heart since that conversation. *Will my parents decide not to let me ride anymore?* The thought made her heart crack in two. *I think it would kill me.*

"Chancy, there you are. Can you grab the blanket that fell

behind the gate?" Nick's voice pulled her from the darkness of her mood.

"Sure." Chancy trotted the rest of the way to the corral and bent over to grab the tan saddle blanket from the ground and passed it through the opening between the rails.

The horse in the corral was wild eyed and breathing hard. A fine sheen of sweat covered the animal's hide. "Where'd you get this one?" she asked, curious. She'd never seen the buckskin on the ranch before. As she wondered who owned the horse, Nick turned his back to the animal when it struck out at him with its front hooves.

"Nick!" she screamed. But to late. The horse's front hoof struck his back and his face scrunched in pain. He fell to the ground and had the good mind to roll before the horse struck again.

"Hurry!" Chancy grabbed his arm and helped pull him from the corral. "Are you all right?" She grasped his shoulders and stared into his face.

"I've been better," Nick finally answered, with a quick swipe to remove the sweat and dirt from his brow. "That's a wild one. I'll have to take it a little slower with her."

"Who's horse is it? She wanted to kill you, looks like she still wants to rip you to shreds by the glint in her eye." Chancy released her grip on his arm and reached for the top rail of the corral. She gave the mare a good once over. The horse paced the enclosure, shaking her black mane and stomping the earth with her front hooves. Madder than an angry polecat.

"You've got your work cut out with her," Chancy grimaced.

"Yes, but your pa brought her to me the other morning. He took her from the buyer in town before he and Deacon left to check on that stud. I was informed she'd been locked in a stall at the back of the sale barn because no one could touch her. The seller wanted her out of his hair. Your pa figured if I can reach her and make her manageable, she'd make a great broodmare. Just look at her, she's beautiful."

That was no lie, the horse had a coppery sleek hide, her black mane and tail were long and thick, a small white star graced her forehead. What wasn't attractive was her attitude. Even now, the mare watched them ears pinned against her neck, an evil glint in her eye.

"Think someone's mistreated her?" Chancy wondered aloud.

"Possibly, she has some scars on her hindquarters, like someone's lashed her a few times in the past. I'm going to just take things slow and easy. I think she'll come around."

Chancy watched Nick enter the corral once more."Be careful," she called.

The gate snapped shut with him never dropping his gaze from the horse's violent stare. He spoke in quiet tones to soothe her and then waved his arms in the air. The mare took off in a run, with a kick of her back legs, in a show of defiance. Nick pushed her forward using his body language. His frame remained square at her shoulder, his eyes never leaving hers. Around and around she went.

"She's starting to soften—watch as she lowers her head. Look at that!"

Chancy's heart leaped with the excitement in Nick's voice. The mare now licked her lips, and her body relaxed.

"Here's the true test. When I drop eye contact, let's see if she will come willingly to me."

Nick turned his head. The mare slowed to a trot, then fell into a walk.

"Let me know if she's going to charge me again." Nick then turned his back to the horse. She came to a stop, ears pointed at Nick like an arrow. She snorted and stomped a foot on the ground.

"Steady, Nick, she's going to come up to you," Chancy said, a little above a whisper.

Nick kept his eyes trained on hers. They were the deepest blue she'd ever seen and when he was with the horses, they twinkled with delight. A streak of dried mud ran down his cheek. *Nick's version of warpaint,* she thought with a smile.

Nick returned her smile, his face full of triumph.

"Let's see if she'll let me touch her now." Nick turned slow, so not to spook her. He reached his hand toward her shoulder. The mare snorted and backed away a few steps, but didn't threaten to bite or strike out at him.

"Easy, girl," he cooed. With gentle movements, he rubbed his palms over her face, her neck, across her shoulder toward her belly. All the while she stood patient, ears pointed in his direction.

"Can you believe this? I wondered if she'd ever let me near her. That's enough for today girl, we'll work on this a little more tomorrow."

Chancy held the gate open for Nick as he walked through. His smile melted her heart, and when he touched her shoulder, a jolt of excitement zipped through her bloodstream.

"I have a surprise for you." He gave her a devilish grin.

Her heart beat faster. "A surprise—you have to tell me." Chancy bit her lower lip to keep from jumping up and down.

"Wait here a second while I put this mare in the other enclosure."

Chancy watched Nick as he reentered the corral. He didn't make eye contact with the mare and stayed near the rail. He then open a second gate leading into a paddock. The mare sensed what he asked and ran past into the open area.

"Good girl," he called after her while he relatched the gate once more.

"Okay, ready for your surprise?"

"Yeees!" She gripped the wood railing.

"Come in here and stand in the middle like I did earlier." Nick pointed his finger at her and waited for her to join him.

Chancy did as he asked.

"I'll be right back." Nick disappeared outside the corral once more. When he returned, he led a sorrel colt at his heels.

"My father send this one to?" she asked.

"Yep, another colt the owner didn't want. You're going to

use my method on this boy and see how it works for you."

Chancy loved nothing better than a challenge. To be able to show Nick she was just as able as he was to work with a horse and make it ridable.

"I'd love to."

Nick took the halter off the colt, and the horse ran to the farthest corner of the corral.

"Okay, you need to push the horse forward with direct eye contact. It's fight or flight for a horse, and they'll normally take to flight."

The warmth of Nick's hands on her shoulders sent a flood of wonderful sensations through her. *Concentrate,* she chided herself for not listening to his instruction. With a deep calming breath, she shook away the little sparks that danced in her veins and instead concentrated on moving the horse forward. It worked. With Nick's patient instruction she had the horse responding to her cues after just a few minutes.

"My god, this is the most wonderful feeling." Chancy turned and threw herself into Nick's arms. His embrace was strong and solid to her. *Oh my goodness, what have I done?* Chancy glanced past Nick, past the corral. Anna stood at the gate, a hateful expression on her face. Never had she felt so deceitful. She stared at the ground in shame and stepped away from Nick.

Nick turned around. Anna's back was to them. "Anna, wait. Come back. Did you see how well Chancy worked this new colt?" Nick called out. She stopped and turned to face them. The hard stare of Anna's brown eyes increased her guilt.

"Chancy's a natural isn't she?" Anna replied, a tight smile on her lips. "Maybe I should have a few lessons too."

"Well if you would like, I'd be happy to help you." Nick looked at Chancy, his eyebrows were drawn together in confusion.

"I'll stop by tomorrow after my chores and see if you're available." Anna left them then with a smirk on her face.

Turmoil rumbled in Chancy's stomach. Anna was her friend, she knew how Anna felt about Nick. She wasn't sure what to say to him now. When she glanced up, he stared into her face. Pride shown on his tan features.

"I knew you could do it all along. I think this technique will work well with your mustang colt."

Chancy's face was heated with embarrassment, but she nodded. "Thanks for everything, Nick. I appreciate all your help." And she did. With Nick at her side, her dreams of capturing the colt and showing her father she was as capable as the other hands in the running of the ranch seemed within reach. Only now, in the process, she'd managed to lose her friend.

CHAPTER SEVEN

"Nick, will you teach me how to throw a lasso?" Nick turned his face, so Anna couldn't see his expression. Anna was beginning to consume a good portion of his time as of late. She showed up every afternoon and followed him like a shadow until he completed whatever chores he'd been assigned for the day. Her nonstop chatter made his head spin. She was a complete opposite of Chancy. Sometimes he'd wondered if he'd get a word out of Chancy when they were together. But the silence between them was comfortable, not obnoxious, or rude.

"Nick, will you also saddle a horse for me today? I'd love for you to go on a ride with me," Anna asked, her dark lashes batting in his direction.

"Sure, but just a short one today." Nick realized several days prior, after the first day of helping her, she'd set her sights on him being her next conquest. Though a nice girl, she had a reputation with the hands. Nick overheard several of the men who'd claimed to have tasted her sweet berry colored lips.

Pretty as she was, she didn't have the effect on him like Chancy did. And he didn't plan on letting himself become her *next* conquest, as some of the men already called him.

They rode out into the rocky region of the ranch. The land was covered in sagebrush and rock formations of various sizes. Anna's voice swarmed like a beehive around his head. The girl could talk nonstop.

"Didn't you hear what I just said?" Anna asked. He turned to her. He'd been lost in thought over Chancy and missed what she'd asked. Anna was a nice girl and his company for the afternoon. He needed to focus on her.

"Sorry, I was gazing off into the distance. There have been wild horses around lately, and I was just hoping to catch a glance."

"You and Chancy really are two peas in a pod, as my mother would say."

"What?" Nick asked.

"All you two ever talk about is horses. When any other topic is mentioned, you both get a far away look on your face and disappear into your heads."

"Oh, sorry, Anna. I hadn't meant to ignore you on purpose." Nick realized his actions were not that of a gentleman. He needed to pay attention to his friend. No matter how exacerbating she could be.

"What are your plans for the future?" he decided to ask.

"Oh, I plan on getting married in the next couple of years. I hope to have a passel of kids. I love children. I'm an only child and sometimes it can be so lonely. Chancy is the closest thing to a sister I've ever had."

Nick cringed. "Quite ambitious, I hope you're able to find yourself a good man to make you happy."

"I plan on it." She smiled. "There's a church social coming up in a few weeks, I was hoping you'd ask me."

Heat climbed Nick's neck. Nothing worse than being put on the spot. He liked Anna all right.

But...she wasn't Chancy. *I've got to stop doing this.* Chancy wasn't for him. In fact, most days she acted like she could barely tolerate him. Only in the last few weeks had she begun to warm up to him.

"Sure," he finally replied. "I'd be happy to take you."

On the ride back, Nick listened to Anna's tales of all the townsfolk. Her lips flapped faster than a hummingbird when it came to talking about people. She was a solid book of knowledge full of tittle-tattle, that was clear.

Chancy was at the barn, grooming Bowie when they returned. Nick noticed the surprised look on her face when she saw Anna at his side. Guilt gnawed at his core, and he wasn't sure why.

"Guess who's taking me to the church social?" Anna

squealed with delight.

Chancy's face paled, and a grimace formed on her lips. Nick swore a pained expression flashed in her eyes.

"That's wonderful, Anna. You'll make a nice couple." With those words she turned and walked away.

"I'll take care of the horses, Anna. Thanks for the ride today." Nick hoped she'd leave. The need to explain to Chancy what was happening ate at his conscience. He sighed with relief when Anna took his suggestion, and with a flirtatious wave sauntered away.

Nick's stomach churned. He wiped a bead of sweat from his brow before walking the horses inside the barn. He could see Chancy in the distance, at her normal spot by Bowie's stall. Only, today, she didn't lead the mare out for a ride. He noticed her shoulders shook and her head rested against the stall door. *She's upset.* His heart dropped to his stomach.

"Chancy, what's wrong?" he asked and placed a hand on her shoulder. It quavered beneath his touch. She didn't answer, so he removed his hand. Unsure what to say, for a crying girl was out of his realm of expertise, he stepped away. He would leave her alone until she was ready to talk.

As he started to walk away, he heard a muffled response from behind.

"I'll be leaving soon."

Nick turned, unsure if he'd heard her correctly.

"Leaving? Where?"

"My ma told me today. We're leaving the ranch in the morning. We'll be visiting her aging aunt in California, then we'll travel by train to Nebraska, to visit her sister, my aunt, and cousins in the city. Omaha. Ma said it would give me better exposure to the culture of the city. Oh Nick, I don't want to go. I can't go. I have a colt to catch."

Nick rubbed his temple. Chancy's departure to Omaha was sudden for sure. It would set her back in her goals. He wasn't sure how to console her on this. It was her parent's decision to take her back east. There was nothing he could do for her.

"I'm sorry. I know how much catching the colt means to you." He paused. "Is there anything I can do to help?"

Chancy looked into his eyes. Her's were still glassy with tears, but they were filled with her usual spirit once more. Her brows furrowed in concentration.

"No, there's nothing you can do to help me while I'm gone. But, when I get back, I'll have to work twice as hard and fast. Will I be able to count on you then?"

"I'll help you however I can, I promise. And Chancy—about Anna."

Chancy raised her hand to stop him. "You don't have to explain anything, Nick..." She turned toward Bowie so he couldn't see her face. "Anna's been sweet on you from the moment you set foot on the ranch. All the cowboys fall for her charms, and I expect you're no different."

Frustration flared like a hot flame in his gut. "Anna's a sweet girl, but I don't have those type of feelings for her," he called out. It was too late, Chancy had left him without a wayward glance on her way back to the ranch house.

***

Nick never thought he'd feel lonesome from the absence of a girl. Chancy in particular. She'd been a daily bystander in the beginning. She'd sit quiet, a long frown on her usually animated features while she clung to the fence rail and he worked her father's horses. Like a flower, she opened up and talked to him in a civilized manor. Thank goodness. He'd felt a connection with her unlike anything he'd experienced before. Like the horses he worked, Chancy yielded and responded to his kindness and showed subtle signs of trust.

There had been a distinct tension in her from the moment they met. The cold hard glint in her eye every time their gazes met. He'd learned real quick Chancy was loving and loyal to three things in her life: her family, her horse, and the ranch. She was knowledgeable and well educated for a girl. This ranch was her life, and its roots ran deep in her soul.

Nick was an outsider here. He'd only wanted a job to

make enough money to stash away and buy his own land to homestead someday. Yet, Chancy's father had made him comfortable, like he was a part of the family. Spoke to him the same as if he was a son, invited him to the house for dinners, asked his advice on the horses. Things which would make his only daughter upset, for it took his attentions away from her.

Nick saw the love she harbored for this land. He couldn't begrudge her that. She'd been born and raised here, the land flowed through her veins. She'd be a fish out of water if she ever had to leave this glorious place. He could only imagine how she must be responding to the city life she'd been thrust into right now.

Finished for the evening, Nick walked to the barn to check the horses once more. He breathed deeply. The familiar smells of the barn: hay, leather, and horse soothed him. He strode toward Bowie's stall. There was an unspoken truce and duty to his friend to care for her horse while she was away.

He brushed the horse's soft coat; the horse relaxed and basked in his attentions. Images of Chancy kept popping into his mind. The way her face lit up each day when she walked to the barn. The look on her face from her bedroom window each morning. He could see her looking out, watching intent as the men went about their day. *I need to stop this, I'll be moving on in no time.*

"Howdy there, cowboy."

The soft timbre voice behind him he recognized immediately. Anna. He turned and noticed she strode toward him. A soft smile on her lush lips, her long dark hair about her shoulders. Nick couldn't deny she was a beautiful girl. She just didn't catch his attention as deeply as Chancy did.

"Hi, Anna. What are you doing out here this time of night?" He took a step out of her reach. It didn't work, her warm hand clutched his upper arm.

"I saw you leave the dining hall and hoped you'd like to take a stroll."

She looked at him, her brown eyes shining, her cheeks

were flushed and a smile graced her lips.

"Well..." he stammered. He didn't want to be rude, but a stroll with Anna wasn't what he had planned for his evening.

"Please?" she begged, brushing her feminine body against him.

Nick groaned inwardly. *No,* his mind screamed. But the gentleman he was said he needed to do this or appear rude.

"Okay, sure." He hated himself for giving in to her charms. He'd need to set his intentions straight with Anna. Not let her go on believing there was a chance for a potential relationship. Anna wrapped her arm through his while they walked along the corrals. Anna chattered about this and that, he found himself unable to say anything.

"I'm so excited about the church social next week," she prattled on, "Nick, do you like to dance?"

"I'm not real experienced to tell you the truth. I've only been to one dance. When I was seventeen, I attended a ball in Boston. I remember not being terribly adept at it."

"Oh, well I can teach you. Really, the dance moves aren't hard at all. We'll have so much fun." Her voice was filled with excitement.

The knot in Nick's stomach grew, and he fought to keep his expression neutral. The church social sounded like torture to him. A short time later they returned to the barn.

"Thanks for the walk, Nick. I enjoyed your company." Anna stood on her tippy-toes and kissed his cheek. Then she twirled around and scurried down the drive toward her parent's house. Nick watched her go in silence.

***

Nick stepped into the bunkhouse. Chet and Slim sat at the table deep in concentration over a game of cards. They glanced up at him with his entrance. Chet was a quiet, aloof cowboy who kept to himself most of the time. His hooded dark eyes missed nothing. Nick was surprised that he'd be involved in a game with Slim.

"How was your walk?" Slim grinned and gave him a wink.

"Fine," Nick replied and walked on by.

Slim was the outgoing, jokester of the bunch. He was quick to smile and liked to tell jokes, and to Nick's enjoyment along with the others, he knew how to play a mean fiddle. He ignored the man's snigger when he walked by.

"Want to join in, Stone?" Slim gave him a cocky smile. His green eyes sparkled with amusement.

"No, thanks, not tonight. I think I'll turn in early." Nick reached his bunk at the far end of the room. He shared a bunk with Jesse, the oldest of the men in the room. Jesse was a quiet, Bible reading cowboy, who when not on the back of a horse, had his nose shoved between the pages of his well worn Bible. Jesse preferred the bottom bunk, so Nick climbed the rungs to reach his mattress at the top.

"Better watch out for Anna," Slim called out. "She's sweet as pie, but switches men faster than her dresses."

"Anna's just a friend, that's all," Nick replied.

"Suure," Chet and Slim responded in unison.

Nick refused to take the bait from their teasing. He laid his head on his pillow and crossed his arms over his chest while staring at the ceiling. Laughter ensued from Slim, and Chet threw down his cards.

"I'm done for the night. It's time to turn in." Chet stood and stretched his limbs, and with spurs jingling at his heels stepped over to the bunk he shared with Slim.

Nick glanced around the room. The bunkhouse was nice quarters compared to some he'd encountered in the past. There was a cozy stove in the corner, a small kitchen and icebox for the men. If they grew hungry during the day or night they could swing in and make a quick bite to eat.

A table was placed in the middle, a bookshelf off to the left. The third bunk set on the other side of the room. There, Don and Bart shared a space. Both men were in their thirties and considered wiry old cowpokes. They liked to ride to town on the weekends and visit the local saloon and dance with the hall girls.

Don and Bart had invited him along several times, but he'd declined. He already learned his lesson in the past with saloons. They sported nothing but hotheads and trouble in most cases. Things Nick preferred to avoid.

The room quickly quieted as the men readied for the next day. Ranch work was hard and laborious. The men woke before first light and were in bed just before dark. Slim blew out the lone candle, and the room became dark. This was Nick's favorite time, he could relax on the soft blankets and dream of his future. Only tonight, Chancy kept sneaking into his thoughts. He sighed and rolled to his side. Snores could be heard below. He squeezed his eyes shut and fell into a dreamless slumber.

***

Chancy stood next to her mother on the busy sidewalk near the bustling train depot in the city of Oakland, California. Folks brushed by them at a frantic pace. She breathed in the distinct scents of the city. The sweat of humans, a sweet yeasty odor from a bakery down the street, and the choking smell of coal from the train.

"We'll be boarding the train in a few minutes. Isn't this exciting, Chancy?" Alma's face was bright with excitement.

Chancy grimaced. "Why's everyone in such a hurry? I've never seen anything like it." Chancy looked around as scores of people of every shape, size, and ethnicity passed her by. There were folks whose skin shined dark as night, then people smaller than herself with slanted eyes and strange clothing. It was all she could do to not be rude and stare as these people all marched by.

Chancy and her mother had been away from the ranch for several weeks now. They'd rode the stage to California first; to visit Alma's elderly Aunt Wilda, whose health was starting to fail. They'd spent the night with Wilda in her small apartment. Wilda was a very sweet lady, who her mother told her was in her late seventies.

Wilda's pale face was covered in wrinkles, but her moss green eyes sparkled with life. Unfortunately, her hearing was nonexistent. Chancy's voice was raw from speaking so loud. After she'd gone to bed, her mother had stayed awake with her and they'd visited late into the night. This morning, Aunt Wilda kissed their cheeks and sent them out the door with a hug. Now, they prepared to board the train. They'd be riding the rails for the next few days on their trip to Nebraska.

"Oh, this is wonderful isn't it, Chancy? It's been years since I've traveled such a distance. And you'll be able to meet your Aunt Bethany, and your cousins, Mary and Cordelia. Maybe some of their ways will rub off on you, and you'll be more interested in what becoming a woman means."

I doubt that, but Chancy kept those words inside. She hated the travel so far. The long days in a dusty stagecoach, being jostled along mile after mile. Then, the scare of the outlaw when they'd entered California. A notorious highwayman, Black Bart, had recently held up several stagecoaches along the stretch of road they'd traveled. The craziest part of the whole situation was how excited her mother was over all this. Chancy would bet her horse if her father had known about Black Bart holding up stages, they'd never been allowed to leave the ranch. Chancy wasn't even permitted to carry a weapon for protection on this trip.

"All aboard." A man dressed in a blue uniform waved the crowd forward. Everyone gathered in a line, and slowly, Alma and Chancy made their way to the entrance of the train. The conductor helped them step up the metal steps and escorted them into the car.

"Over here, dear. We'll be able to watch the scenery from the window as we travel." Alma reached for her elbow and ushered her toward the seat she wanted.

Chancy took the window seat. Outside, people walked by in groups. A tall, well dressed black man carried a traveling case in each arm and followed a short plump well-to-do looking white woman with a passel of children. Chancy had never realized there were so many people in the world.

The seat was hard against her back and bottom as she settled in. She wiggled around on the hard solid platform, called a seat, to make herself more comfortable. Heat from her mother's side warmed her. "I have snacks in my satchel if you're feeling hungry, Chancy. Or, if you'd like to read, Aunt Wilda let us borrow a couple books which we can return when we come home."

"Ma, I think I'll just rest, it's been a long day." Chancy lay her head back and closed her eyes. It would be a long week.

***

Chancy had never felt so constricted in her life. The rail car was worse than a prison. Her bottom was raw and numb from sitting for so long. Her back ached and her head throbbed. The past three weeks of travel, in her mind, had been hell. She cringed at the term, but couldn't find one more suitable.

"Aunt Bethany's arranged for someone to wait for us at the train depot in Omaha," her mother informed her. Chancy held back a sigh over her mother's apparent excitement.

"I can't wait," Chancy replied. But the idea of standing on solid ground once again did improve her spirits.

"Soon as we arrive in Omaha, your Aunt Bethany will have an escort take us directly to her townhouse. I bet you're excited to meet your cousins, Cordelia and Mary," her mother prattled on.

"Mary will be married at the end of summer. Cordelia, she's only a couple years older than you, Chancy. Bethany said the girls can't wait to meet you."

What would these city folk cousins of hers be like she wondered? Already in her mind, she could picture them from the descriptions her mother had given. Fancy dresses, upturned chins. Would they want anything to do with the broom-tail chasing, uncivilized country cousin of theirs? The thought brought a smile to her lips. *Who cares, we'll only be here a week. What's another week out of my life to make my parents happy.*

***

Two hours later, Chancy and her mother stepped inside the well-to-do home of Bethany Mannings. Her aunt was widowed, her deceased husband an up-and-coming doctor before his untimely demise from consumption.

"Alma!" A thin woman with deep brown hair piled upon her head rushed at them. "Bethany," her mother called meeting her aunt in the middle of the spacious room.

"You ladies must be exhausted! Jim," she called. A man dressed in a dark brown suit stepped into the room behind them and grabbed their two traveling cases.

"This way, ladies." His heavy Irish brogue surprised Chancy. She'd never heard such a thick accent before. Too tired to ponder further, both she and her mother followed close behind.

They were led up a magnificent staircase. The dark wood was smooth under her hand and polished till it gleamed. The room at the top of the stairs was open and spacious. Paintings hung from the walls, and a window was open at the far end, to let a cool breeze flow through. Along the hall five closed doors came into view.

"Ladies, your room will be the last one on the left."

Chancy and her mother followed Jim inside. The room was painted a soft blue with lacy white curtains framing a large open window. A dark blue quilt covered the large bed. A dresser and mirror were placed along the wall.

"Mrs. Mallory, this will be your room." Jim turned to Chancy. "Charlotte, Cordelia has asked if you'll room with her. She's most excited to meet you."

Not used to being called Charlotte by anyone, she missed the part of rooming with her cousin. A shot of trepidation washed through her. *What if I don't like her?*

"You're here!" Female voices could be heard outside the door just before two young women stormed into the room. Before her stood her proclaimed cousins. They appeared vivacious girls her age with matching expressions of delight.

Suddenly shy and unsure of herself, Chancy gave the girls a small smile.

"Where's her bag, Jim? Bring it to my room. Charlotte come with us." With no room for argument, her cousins each grabbed her by an arm and whisked her out of the room.

"Go on, Chancy, I'll catch up with you later," her mother called from behind her.

"How was your journey? Oh, we're so excited to finally meet you." Both girls looked her over with wide eyed interest.

"I have to admit, we were expecting a freckle faced tomboy, not someone as pretty as you." Her cousin Cordelia, the more vocal of the two stated. The girl's intense stare brought a flush to Chancy's cheeks.

"Well..." before Chancy could comment, Mary stepped forward and touched her hair.

"That color is the deepest, richest brown, I've ever seen."

"Thank you," Chancy stammered. "You both are a little different from what I expected too."

"Really?" Cordelia looked abashed. "What did you think we'd be like?

Chancy blushed that much more. She'd never admit to the sisters what she really thought they'd be like.

"Never mind, Charlotte we're going to have so much fun while you're here. We've been invited to a ball at the end of the week, and you're invited. Do they have balls back in Oregon?" Cordelia asked, her eyebrows raised in curiosity.

Chancy cleared her throat. "I go by Chancy. I don't recognize myself as Charlotte. And no, we don't have balls. We do have church socials. I haven't been to any though, with work at the ranch..."

Her cousins stared at her in shock.

"You've never been to a dance? Never felt a young beau's arms around you, warm and sweet as he twirls you around the dance floor?" Cordelia floated around the room in an imaginary partner's arms before stopping in front of her. Both sisters shook their heads. Their eyes bulged, and they wore matching expressions of mock horror on their young faces.

"No, I haven’t." A little spark of anger lit in her gut. She wouldn't be bowled over by these girls, family or not.

Wide smiles lit both girl's faces. "Well, we'll fix that for sure this week." Mary stated, matter of fact.

"You mean to tell me a girl pretty as you has no beau back home?" Cordelia placed her hands on her hips, an odd look came over her features. "Have you ever been kissed?"

Before Chancy could answer, for she was to tongue tied and flustered at the moment, Aunt Bethany and her mother came to her rescue.

"Cordelia, what are you doing to this poor child. She must be exhausted, and here you are quizzing her on beaus. Let the poor girl rest."

"Yes, mother." Cordelia had the good sense to look abashed by her directness.

Chancy glanced at her aunt with relief. Suddenly, she was tired, and the bed covered in a thick quilt looked like heaven about now.

"Chancy, we'll leave you to rest awhile. When you wake, we have so much to show and tell you. We'll be downstairs in the living room when you're ready."

"Thanks," Chancy replied, relieved she'd have a few moments to herself.

The two sisters, her Aunt Bethany and her mother all left. The quietness of the room relaxed her. She sat on the thick blue and green quilt covering the bed. Once her boots were off, she curled into a ball on the mattress and was soon fast asleep.

CHAPTER EIGHT

Chancy awoke with a start and stared at the ceiling. Her dream was still vivid and full of life in her mind. Nick walked toward a horse, hidden in the shadows of a corral. *Snowbar.* No, he wouldn't go against her wishes and capture her horse on his own. *He knows how much that horse means to me.*

She sat up on the edge of the bed. The room was full of shadows from the fading sun. With a heavy sigh she smoothed out the wrinkles which had formed on her dress. A cool breeze from the window brushed against her face. Chancy stood and walked over to the window to peer out. A familiar process she repeated at home each morning.

At this house, the window faced a busy street at the edge of a wide, green lawn. Elaborate carriages with drivers dressed in black, wearing fancy hats passed by. Women holding parasols and wearing lavish dresses which flared out behind them with ruffles and lace strolled leisurely by.

Entranced by this odd assortment of activities, the knock at the door didn't phase her.

"You awake, Chancy?" It was her mother's voice.

"Yes—I just woke up." The door cracked open, and her mother stepped inside. Her face still alight with the excitement of being in the city, Chancy was sure. She'd never seen her mother so carefree.

"I hope you enjoy your time here. I wanted to show you a different lifestyle from what you're used to. Show you there is an easier life than the one we live."

"Ma, I love the life we have on the ranch. I couldn't imagine not living that life. Being here is like a strange dream to me. I feel like an outsider looking in."

Alma stepped forward and wrapped her arms around her

shoulders in a comforting embrace.

With her chin resting on Chancy's head she gave her a gentle squeeze. "Your father and I are proud of you Chancy, don't ever forget that."

"Thanks, Ma." Her mother's words eased the burden she forever carried in her heart. The need to prove herself over and over. For even though she was a girl she was made of the same tough, courageous bloodlines all Mallorys came from.

"Your cousins are downstairs waiting for you, go join them and enjoy yourself."

"Thank you." Chancy returned her mother's hug and raced out the door.

The dark mahogany staircase was cool under her hand on her way to the bottom floor. She reminded herself to act a lady, and take each step, one at a time, instead of the two she'd take if she was alone.

The home was richly decorated with elaborate artwork. Pieces which were strange to the eye, Chancy thought upon further examination. The paintings were full of varying colors and shapes and made no sense in her mind. Fine china vases and bowls were spread throughout. Her cousins had a footman, a maid, and a cook in their home she'd been informed by her mother earlier.

Cordelia spotted her first when she entered the living room. "You're awake!" She and Mary stood from their seats and stepped forward. An older woman stood behind them, a stern expression on her features.

"Chancy, this is our escort, Nettie," Cordelia explained.

The older woman, with dark brown hair tinged with specks of silver stepped forward and extended her hand.

"It's nice to meet you, Chancy. The girls have talked non-stop about you since your arrival earlier today."

Chancy took the older woman's cool hand in her own. Nettie had a firm grip and shook her hand with purpose. Chancy looked into her stone gray eyes. A small light of amusement burned in her black orbs.

"We've talked with mother, and she said it would be all right to take you to our dressmaker and have you fitted for a gown. One so grand all our friends will be jealous at the ball," Cordelia's voice brimmed with excitement.

"I think her gown should be a shade of deep blue. She'd look ravishing in that hue," Mary commented. Her index finger rested against her chin while she stared at Chancy.

"Oh yes, blue will be marvelous on her," Cordelia agreed. Her cousins' spoke in excited tones as they led her out the front door and down the cobbled walk to an awaiting carriage. Two sleek, gray horses stood at attention. Chancy paused to admire their glossy appearance. Their harnesses were black and were oiled till they gleamed. The driver, dressed in a dark suit and top hat, smiled at her.

"These are beautiful horses," she commented.

"Thank you, miss, they're Standardbreds. Mr. Mannings used to have a stable full of these beauties. But, when he passed...well, Mrs. Mannings only kept a few." The man quieted and assisted them into the carriage compartment. They were whisked away at a brisk trot. Chancy watched out the small window while they passed other carriages in the road. Her thoughts still on the beautiful horses her cousin's family owned.

"Chancy, do you have plans for the summer?" Cordelia asked.

Her attempt at polite conversation with the question set Chancy on edge. Her cousins would never understand her love of the land in Oregon. Chasing wild horses, running with Bowie across an open field, the wind blowing through her hair. The smell of fresh sweet grass in the air. Her cousins would be horrified by such behavior. Just like she was horrified by going to this ball for goodness sakes.

"The summer is a busy time of year on our ranch. I love to help the ranch hands break the new colts. Then, we have a roundup for branding the calves, and in the fall my pa lets the men choose a colt from the mustang herds that cross through our ranch."

"Well, what about boys? Don't you have social events out west where you can dress up and flirt with boys?" Cordelia asked with a touch of horror in her voice.

"Chancy, I honestly can't believe you don’t have a beau. Are you holding back on us?" Mary's direct gaze bit into her.

"Well..."Chancy decided to choose her words carefully. The image of Nick popped into her mind. He was not even close to being a beau, but if she embellished their working relationship just a tad, then maybe the sisters would leave her alone. *If I'm lucky,* she shook her head.

"Do tell, do tell," the sisters voices echoed in sync. Their escort, Nettie stared at her also. A look of knowing crossed her eloquent features.

Chancy cleared her throat, her face flushed, and a sweat broke out on her forehead. "His name is Nick Stone. He's my father's new ranch hand."

"Nick Stone," Cordelia let the name roll off her little, pink tongue. The way she spoke his name aloud made Chancy want to slap her face. "What a strong name." She sighed. "Is he handsome? Oh he must be with a name like that." She batted her eyelashes.

"Go on—I'm dying for you to tell us what he looks like." Mary jumped in.

"Well..." Chancy started. "He's tall and slim as most cowboys are. His face is tan from hours in the saddle under the sun's direct rays, and his eyes are blue as the Oregon sky. He doesn't talk much, which is a blessing, and he's excellent with horses." A smile formed on her lips."'Knows how to make them do what he wants and make it seem as if it was their idea.' Those are my pa's words." Pride swelled in Chancy's heart. The sound of those words from her lips—changed the way she'd thought of Nick. Her face flushed a shade deeper. The realization she cared for Nick shook her to her core.

"Ladies, we're at the Donner's Dress shop." The carriage driver called down to them. The carriage came to a halt. Chancy was escorted with her cousins, who chattered nonstop with their motherly escort into the shop.

Inside, scores of dresses of every fashion and color imaginable hung from wire hangers and figurines. Yards of fabrics of every texture lined the walls. Never, had Chancy seen so much elegance.

"Mrs. Donner, this is our cousin, Charlotte, excuse me, 'Chancy' Mallory. From the west coast. She's in need of a dress by the end of the week for the upcoming ball." Mary stepped forward to introduce them.

"Why Charlotte, you have such natural beauty. A true flower of the west. Come here child, and we'll see what we can do." Mrs. Donner waved her forward.

Chancy took a hesitant step. The woman grabbed a measuring string from the table and began wrapping it around her waist, her arms and chest.

"I think a deep shade of blue would do your complexion nicely."

"My thoughts exactly." Mary clapped her hands together in excitement.

Chancy held in a groan, while the woman and her cousins' spoke of her complexion and waistline like she wasn't standing in front of them at all.

"Chancy, we never got a chance to ask. Has your Nick whispered sweet words in your ear? Has he brought your wrist to his lips and kissed the tender flesh there?" Cordelia asked, pointing to her own wrist, a mischievous glint in her eye.

"Cordelia, you're making her blush, stop this questioning." Nettie reprimanded the sisters.

Chancy turned her back to the lot of them and took a deep breath. Images she'd never thought imaginable raced through her mind. Nick holding her in his arms. Nick's blue eyes staring into her own as he leaned in closer and closer...

Suddenly, she missed him with great intensity. So much so she missed the rest of the conversation in the room.

"I didn't mean to embarrass her, I remember my first kiss.

Two summers ago, Thomas Higgin's grabbed me aside out in the garden and kissed the heavenly daylights out of me. How can a girl ever forget a kiss such as that? And, I hope every girl gets one as memorable," Cordelia finished, hand placed over her heart, a dreamy look still in her eyes.

"All right, ladies, I believe I have everything I need. Come back on Wednesday, the dress shall be ready then." Mrs. Donner smiled, her white teeth shining in the light.

Once more, they were hustled into the carriage, Nettie at their heels and returned to the manor house. The evening ended after a delicious dinner of exotic foods Chancy had never tasted before.

Roast lamb with herbed potatoes, corn cakes and for dessert a delicious ice cream.

They retired to the library after dinner. Chancy sat on the luxurious leather couch beside her mother. Her Aunt Bethany sat on the couch facing them with Cordelia and Mary next to her. Chancy was lulled into a peaceful slumber with the lively conversation around her. Her eyelids drooped, and a warm and fuzzy sensation filled her.

"Chancy, why don't you go on to bed, tomorrow will be a fresh day with plenty of time to visit."

Her aunt's words were a godsend. "Thank you, I think I will."

"So soon?" Cordelia called out. "We have so much to plan for the ball."

"There's still plenty of time this week to make plans for the ball," her aunt interrupted.

Chancy retired to her borrowed bed and was asleep before her head could hit the pillow.

***

The rest of the week flew by without a moment to worry about being homesick. Though
Chancy realized Nick was never far from her mind, during this trip she had learned something about herself; Nick was now an important part of her life. Anna would just have to understand.

Much to her horror, Friday, the day of the ball, came all too soon. Her cousins had flitted about in a frenzy of preparations. In her week at this household, she'd come to the conclusion she'd never be a city girl. The dresses were too tight and confining, the airs one put on around folks was offensive and overall being inside all day just about killed her.

She missed Bowie, as much, if not more than the wide opens spaces of her family's sprawling ranch. But knowing she and her mother would be leaving for home on Sunday gave her strength to go on. Two more days. If she could make it through this ball, life would soon be back to normal.

***

Nick spurred his mount into a run across the open meadow. The horse extended his neck, his
stride lengthening. He let himself concentrate on the energy of the horse. The speed, muscles that flexed beneath him. The power. He leaned over the horse's mane, urging the mount faster. Freedom. It was the only word that came to mind and gave him the release he sought.

The end of the meadow came into view, and he pulled back on the reins. His mount slowed to a trot. The mustangs grazed in the distance. A white leopard colt ran in front of the herd, bucking and kicking. Chancy's colt.

He watched the white, speckled colt go through his paces. Chancy had chosen well. Without a backward glance he turned his horse and started for the ranch once more. Soon Chancy would be home, and they could resume their plans and capture the colt.

Chancy was on his mind a lot lately. He missed their conversations. The evening rides they'd taken, her delighted laughter. So much so his plans for the future seemed to have come to a standstill.

He had his own dreams he hoped to fulfill, but he remained planted here at the Mallory ranch.

"What should I do?" he questioned his sanity for staying at this ranch for too long. It was easy to become attached. Get off track on his future plans. *I want my own place like this someday.* With horses grazing in pastures of lush green meadows, cattle, fat and happy, ready to be shipped to market.

The land was vast and full of opportunity. Why is it when I think of the future Chancy is always at my side? This disturbed him, for he barely knew her. What he did know of her had taken over any good sense he may have had.

Back at the ranch, Nick put his horse away for the night. Walking past the last stall, a shadow caught his eye. Was Anna lurking around waiting for him? Curious, he stopped to listen. No, it wasn't Anna. A slight noise could be heard beneath the mound of hay. *Whimpers?*

Nick knelt on his knees for a closer look. A tail, black with a splash of white at the tip wagged back and forth. *A dog?* Nick had never seen a dog on the ranch in the months he'd been here.

"Here, boy," he kept his voice low and gentle. The tail swished faster. Nick parted the hay, and sure enough there was a pup. Big brown eyes stared up at him, and the little body shook in fear.

"Come here, boy. I won't hurt you." Nick gently scooped the warm bundle of fur into his arms. The pup whimpered again, its soft body shaking in his arms. He held the dog up for inspection. He noticed a red stain on the dog's white paw.

"You're hurt, little guy." Holding the pup close to his chest, he carried him to the bunkhouse.

"Whatcha got there?" Slim asked as he stepped through the doorway into the warmth of the room.

"I found this little guy hiding in the haystack inside the barn. I've never seen any dogs on the ranch. Have you guys noticed a dog before?" Nick walked over to the stove. He sat down on the wooden floorboards and placed the pup before him. He wanted to check how severe the dog's injury was.

"I found a dog about a week ago while riding fence-line. It was dead. I figured maybe from old age. The body didn't look like had been hurt or anything, but I didn't get off my horse to check neither.

Wonder if this here pup might have been with it and he decided to follow me back to the ranch?" Chet wondered.

Nick scratched the dog behind the ears and was rewarded with a swipe of the dog's scratchy tongue over his fingers.

"You're in good hands now. Let's get you patched up." Nick held the pup's injured paw and inspected the wound. "Look's like just a scrape. I think you're going to live, little guy."

Nick cleansed the injury with water and wrapped a length of cloth over the dog's foot. The pup bit at the ends of the material.

"Look, he thinks his bandage is a chew toy." Slim laughed. He was right, the pup put great drama into tugging at the fabric. Soon the cloth was removed, and the dog was shaking his snout back and forth.

"Whatcha gonna name the little tike?" Chet asked.

Nick scratched his head. He'd been subconsciously wondering the very same thing.

"Not sure, to tell you the truth." Nick looked the little black and white bundle over. He had a white nose and white around his eyes, a black body and tail until the tip. The pointy end was white too, along with four white paws. The poor animal was skin and bones, Nick noticed. With the loss of his presumed mama, he hadn't eaten much in the last week he suspected.

"I'll call him Bones," he finally answered.

"What kind of name is that?" Chet scoffed.

"I don't know, it just kind of stuck in my mind."

"Bones it is then boys, look at the little guy go." The men sat around and watched the pup with glee. Happier than boys around a Christmas tree while the dog dashed from person to person, spinning out of control on the wood floors.

"I haven't had a pup in years. No time for such nonsense," Jesse commented from behind his Bible. "I can do you a favor and take him on into town and find him a nice home with a couple of kids to play with if you like."

"No, I think I'll keep him." Nick shook his head. "I always

wanted a dog. Now, I guess I have one."

"Well the little guy needs some food in his belly. I think there's some scraps from dinner on the counter that haven't been tossed out yet, better get them," Jesse said, his face hidden behind his Bible once more.

"Thanks, will do." Nick walked over and grabbed the plate which had a few scraps remaining for the dog. The pup scrambled to where Nick set the plate on the floor and dove in.

Once the pup had his belly full, Nick took him outside once more for potty duty before he put him on his bunk. The pup plopped down on the blanket and closed his eyes.

"Night, Bones. Sleep tight, we rise early around here."

After a long night of ups and downs to let the pup out to do his business, Nick drank his coffee down in several gulps. He ignored the burn in his throat and stuffed two biscuits and several chunks of bacon into his jacket, wrapped inside a napkin. He needed to go with Slim today on the south end of the ranch looking for stray cattle.

Nick had fashioned a pack of sorts from a pillow case to bring Bones along with him. He'd be in trouble if he left the pup inside the bunkhouse to chew on the men's belongings while he was out working. It was safer to just bring him along for now, until he became a bit older. Nick could start his training this way anyhow.

"What are you doing to that poor dog?" Slim asked, after Nick had mounted his horse. He had the pack tied around his neck, the pups head stuck out at his chest.

"Bringing Bones along. Today his training begins."

"Why that's the dangest setup I've ever seen." Slim chuckled at him.

"He's still too sore in the paw and weak from no food to have him follow on foot. In a week or so he should be good as new."

"Sounds good, partner. Let's get to work."

The men rode out in silence. The pup let out a yip, ears alert, while he watched from his post at Nick's chest.

CHAPTER NINE

"Time to leave, Chancy," her cousins Mary and Cordelia's voices echoed with equal intensity and elation. Chancy grimaced. The blue satin shoes she was required to wear because they matched her dress pinched her feet already and she hadn't left the room yet.

"Coming," she called back. Her heart beat faster than a runaway horse against her ribcage. *I don't feel like myself in these clothes.* She stared at herself in the floor-length mirror on the wall. The blue gown fit her to perfection, showing each young curve with flattering efficiency. Never, had she wore anything so grand.

"Oh, darling, you look beautiful." Alma stepped into the room. She was dressed in a lavish cream-colored gown, trimmed with tulle and flowers with matching gloves. Chancy had never seen her wear this dress before.

"My... mother..." Chancy was awestruck by her mother's gown and how young and beautiful it made her look.

"Yes, isn't it grand? I made this dress special for this occasion back home. I myself haven't been to a ball since I was young. Your age to be exact. It's one of my fondest memories, other than when I met your father. Now, let's go, everyone is waiting on us." Her mother smiled at her.

Together they walked down the fine staircase and to the parked carriage out front. Mary, Cordelia and Aunt Bethany waited inside the compartment.

"Chancy, you're stunning in that dress." Aunt Bethany complimented her when they were all seated.

Chancy's cheeks became heated. "Thanks," she said, unable to hide the hint of pleasure which warmed her soul. *This must be how a princess feels.*

The chatter was nonstop inside the moving carriage, much to Chancy's relief. She didn't have any desire to take part in the women's endless prattle. Her mind was elsewhere. Images of Nick had haunted her all day. She recalled how strong his arms felt around her when she had taken liberties and thrown herself into his embrace after her excitement with the horses.

She'd been embarrassed by her actions at the time, now she wished she would have pursued things a little further. *A kiss maybe?* Her cousins had definitely rubbed off on her this week. *When was the last time I worried about kissing a boy?* That was her friend Anna's area of expertise.

"We're here! Oh, Chancy, you're going to love this." Mary's words raised her hackles. Already she felt like she'd had enough. *Just a little longer, Sunday, Mother and I will be on our way home once more.*

They were escorted out of the carriage by Jim and led up the stone walk and into the grand white building. The front of the residence was surrounded with fragrant roses. The flowers' thick scent wafted in the breeze when they passed. The building itself was recently painted, the strong odor of paint still lingered.

Inside, was an illustrious hall, rich dark wood floors gleamed from hours of polishing. Men and women in glamorous gowns all seemed to turn their way and stare. Chancy froze. Never had she seen anything so full of opulence. She wondered what someone like herself was doing in a place such as this. The walls seemed to close in around her. She yearned for the open meadows that surrounded her home in Oregon.

"Have your dance card ready, Chancy. I can see several young gentlemen already looking your way," Cordelia told her as she walked away.

Before Chancy had a chance to retort, they were met by an older couple who spoke with her mother and Aunt Bethany. Chancy learned this couple's name was Smith. They had organized this dance in their grand home.

The room was cleared of all furniture, except along the

walls. Chairs were lined for those who wished to sit and rest. At the farthest corner a refreshment table was erected with crystal bowls full of colorful refreshments set atop lavish lace tablecloths.

Chancy breathed deep. The strong smell of women's cologne mixed with that of the men's was overwhelming. She glanced around. There were no windows in the space, only open doors at each side of the room. Claustrophobia moved in.

A small band played a lively waltz across the room from the refreshments, and men and women gathered on the floor to begin the dance. Chancy noted Cordelia on the arm of a handsome gentleman. She seemed to float across the dance floor in his arms. Mary stood off to the side with a group of women, deep in conversation.

Chancy followed her mother and aunt to the table full of refreshments. The table boasted tea, coffee and punch, along with cakes, biscuits, and sandwiches. She poured herself some punch then turned and watched the dancers. Mary was now on the dance floor being whisked around the room by a gentleman dressed in a black suit. They made a fine couple, Chancy thought, while she watched with interest. She was surprised Mary would dance with her upcoming marriage at the end of summer.

"That's a childhood friend, Mark Styles, who Mary dances with," Aunt Bethany replied in answer to her unspoken question.

Cordelia, now stood off to the side, a smile on her face for a new young gentleman who requested a dance from her. Cordelia's dress of white tarlatan flowed about her feet when she returned to the dance floor with her partner. The scene was beautiful to observe, but Chancy couldn't imagine herself out there. But still a little pang of jealousy entered her heart. *Maybe if Nick were here.* She imagined herself in his arms, he, dressed in a black suit as he twirled her around the dance floor. *Stop,* she chided herself on her silliness.

"Will you do me the honor to dance with me?" A young

man who couldn't be much older than herself stood a short distance away, eyeing her speculatively.

Is he talking to me? Chancy glanced around anxiously. There was no one but herself in the vicinity. Her heart skipped a beat, and her breath caught in her chest. He was tall with wide shoulders and eyes black as night, with thick dark hair to match. His smile was wide. He was a handsome sight to behold in a dark way, and she realized she held in a breath. It's only a dance, she told herself and gave the boy a shy smile.

"With pleasure," she answered as her cousins had taught her and extended her gloved hand into his warm one. It was then, Chancy found herself in the strong arms of her partner. He whisked her around the floor with no effort on his part. She clung to his arms letting him lead the way until the music stopped. She found she was breathless when he returned her to her mother's side. He gave a curt bow and a smile before he turned and left her.

"My, that young man is quite the catch, Chancy. How lucky for you he picked you out of all these other girls."

Chancy's face warmed with her mother's words. She glanced in the nameless boy's direction, and he gave her another smile before disappearing into the throngs of people.

"Chancy, do you know who that is?" Her cousin Mary appeared at her side once more full of excitement. "That's Jake O'Connor. His family is the richest in all of Omaha." Her hand tapped her chest, over her heart. He's considered a bit of a rogue around these parts and he rarely dances. For him to choose you..." Mary looked her over, an awed expression on her face.

Cordelia rushed over to them. "Oh, Chancy, how wonderful. All the girls here are furious Jake picked you out of all of us in this room to dance with. He never dances!"

Chancy glanced around the room. It appeared Cordelia was right. Outright glares to looks of clouded suspicion from multitudes of girls and women stared in her direction.

"They have nothing to worry about from me, I'll be leaving Sunday morning." She spoke the words loud enough so those around could hear, then cast a glare of her own to all the ninny's who scorned her over one dance with a handsome boy. This lifestyle was beyond her comprehension.

Much to her discomfort, Jake O'Connor asked for several more dances before the evening was over.

"Where are you from?" His voice was rich, masculine, with a hint of danger wrapped around it.

"From Oregon," she answered with pride. "My family owns a large spread there. We raise horses and cattle. Do you like horses?" she asked.

"Ah, my sweet girl. I'd hate to waste our precious time together boring you with stories of my horses. I own my own stable in this town, haven't you been told?"

His own stable. Chancy ached to speak of him of horses, but was unsure. Society rules here were strict and confusing. It seemed a person had to beat around the bush to get the answers they wanted in a coy and flirtatious way. Which was ridiculous. Chancy had been taught one should get straight to the point. Instead, she floundered around unsure of what to say.

"What's wrong," Jake whispered in her ear as he swung them around the dance floor in accordance with the waltz.

"Would it be too direct to ask what kind of horses you own? Believe me, you won't be boring me, but if you mention luncheons or teas, you might have to hold me up, while I fall asleep in your arms."

Jake laughed, his eyes full of amusement. "You are a breath of sunshine around here, Charlotte."

"No," she stopped him. "Please, call me Chancy. I detest being called Charlotte."

He smiled at her once again. She noticed the look of admiration in his dark eyes. "Chancy it is then. I own a stable full of thoroughbreds which I race in many of the states. My horses are some of the fastest here in the Midwest."

"My father's spoken of thoroughbreds, they are fast, sleek, and hot blooded. Beautiful creatures.

We raise cow ponies. My pa's always on the lookout for

fresh bloodlines to improve our stock. My own horse is a mustang I captured off the range. She's the fastest and smartest horse on our ranch," Chancy stated with pride. Let Jake O'Connor chew on that.

"A broomtail?"

"Did I stutter?" she challenged.

Jake laughed and placed his forehead against her own. "Chancy, you're a girl after my own heart."

"Mustangs are some of the smartest creatures God ever created," she stated. Chancy had no qualms about sticking up for her horse. She'd stake her life on Bowie against any of Jake O'Connor's fancy thoroughbreds. Bowie was cunning, fast, and above all, she knew survival on the lands. Let one of those high class thoroughbreds onto the range and see how long it could last. But, she wasn't here to bet with Jake, nor make an enemy of him. Instead, she gave him a smile.

"Well, Chancy, a woman who's not afraid to talk horseflesh and stand by her ideals. I must say I admire you. Maybe someday I'll come west and visit your ranch. It sounds wild and intriguing. Much like yourself. Could I interest you in a visit to my stables tomorrow? I'd love to talk horses with you a little longer." The dance had ended.

"I'd like that very much." Chancy's heart raced. A chance to visit a prestigious stable with racehorses, how could she turn that down? Jake walked her back to her awaiting family. He reached for her hand and brought it to his lips. Her heart skipped a beat when the heat of his lips touched her skin.

"Thanks for the enjoyable company. I'll have my carriage driver pick you and your family up in the morning, if they too, would like a tour?" Jake glanced past her to her mother and aunt who stood quiet behind her.

"That would be lovely." Chancy returned his smile, a little breathless. He gave her a devilish smile before walking away.

Chancy wasn't sure if she was relieved now that she was out of his clutches or not. She couldn't complain about his company, he had impeccable manners, superior dancing skills, and his appearance was easy on the eyes.

Her cousins' knowing smiles made her uncomfortable. It was as if they knew or suspected something she wasn't aware of and this made her stomach knot. She held her chin high and refused to let the jealous looks in her direction every few minutes by the other girls intimidate her.

When the night was over to her great relief and the proper goodbyes had been completed, all five women collapsed onto the benches inside the carriage. Mary and Cordelia reviewed the night's events. Chancy was too blurry eyed and exhausted to join in the conversation. She rested her cheek on her mother's shoulder and closed her eyes.

"Chancy, we're home." Chancy awoke with a start. *Home?* Could it be they were back at the ranch? But her cousins' soft laughter tinkled in her ears and she remembered they'd just left the ball.

The group left the carriage and were escorted by Jim into the Mannings' house. Chancy, too tired to remove her dress collapsed on the bed. Within moments she was fast asleep.

***

The next morning began with a bustle of activity. When Chancy rose from the bed, her gown a wrinkled mess around her, her first step sent a grimace to her face. Sharp pains radiated up her legs. Her feet had never hurt this bad in her life. The too tight shoes she'd worn the night before had bruised the pads of her feet.

Ignoring the pain, she pulled off the dance gown and donned a simple dress. She'd put on no airs for Jake O'Connor as the other girls in this town did. She did find him intriguing with his dark, handsome looks. But, it was his horses she was most interested in. True thoroughbred racehorses. A chance she might never have again.

Breakfast was torture. "Chancy, you can't wear *that* to the O'Connors. They live in a mansion. Jake's horses' stable is twice as big as our house." Cordelia's face was covered in shock.

"This dress will be fine. I'm not looking for a beau, I'm

going to have a look at his horses."

Chancy couldn't help the smug smile that came to her lips. Her cousins, who would escort her, along with Nettie, wore their finest gowns. The dresses were just as elegant as the gowns they wore the night before.

"Nettie, talk some sense into her quick, before Jake's carriage arrives." Mary cringed beside Cordelia."It will be scandalous otherwise," she added.

"Let her be, girls," Nettie proclaimed. "Chancy is beautiful in any dress she desires to wear. Jake will see the difference."

Both Mary and Cordelia quieted over this. They stared at her with glances full of trepidation. "I guess you're right, she is lovely in a wild sort of way. I think that's why Jake fawns over her.

She's unlike any other girl in the state of Nebraska," Mary stated.

"Ladies, the O'Connor carriage has arrived," Jim announced.

"Off we go, girls. Grab your jackets and hats." Nettie pushed her chair from the table and stood.

Chancy's breakfast remained untouched on her plate. She was too excited to eat. She set her napkin down and joined Cordelia and Mary, who had already left the table and gathered around Nettie by the door.

"Good morning, ladies." Jake O'Connor stood next to his carriage, a wide grin on his lips. He was dressed in black once again, except for the white, crisp shirt he wore under his jacket. His dark eyes flashed with humor. Once again, Chancy was taken aback by his dangerous good looks. His gaze never left her's while he helped Nettie and her cousins into the compartment.

When it was her turn to step inside, Jake grabbed for her hand. "Let me." The soft leather of his glove was warm in her hand. Chancy knew her face was flushing, for the air was crisp minutes earlier and now that same coolness soothed the heat on her cheeks.

"Thank you," were the only words she could squeak out.

She knew her cousins watched her every move like a hawk. Once everyone was inside and comfortable on the padded bench seats, Jake nodded to the driver to move out.

"I thank you ladies for letting me give you a tour of the O'Connor stables. I hope you enjoy the grounds and the beautiful horseflesh that graces the O'Connor property."

"We wish to thank you also, Jake, for this wonderful opportunity. We know Chancy will be forever grateful," Cordelia piped up,"she loves horses. Even has several of her own, we've been told.

One, being a wild mustang she captured from the wilderness and trained herself," she added.

Chancy's cheeks burned a little brighter with her cousin's words.

"So, I've heard." Jake winked at her from across the carriage.

Cordelia looked at her. Her stare was full of question.

Chancy cleared her throat, "I mentioned my horse to Jake last night."

"Oh," Cordelia replied.

"How many horses do you own, Jake?" Mary asked, to ease the sudden discomfort in the carriage, Chancy was sure. There were rules of etiquette at balls, and Chancy feared she may have broke most of them last night in Jake's arms.

"Well over a hundred," he answered.

Mary and Cordelia gasped in union. "Our father had horses before he passed. Our stable held no more than twenty," Mary replied.

"My horses have trainers, caregivers, veterinarians. Their own entourage of workers to keep them fit and primed for racing," Jake stated.

"How many races have you won?" Chancy asked.

"More than I can keep up with. Right now I have seven two-year-olds out on the tracks. Two geldings and five fillies. There's a fine balance with racehorses. You need the right amount of stamina and speed. The rest of my horses consist of several stallions, mares, foals, and geldings. With my breeding program I have in place currently, I hope to have many more wins in my future."

"My, isn't this interesting?" Mary fanned herself. She wore a bored expression on her face.

"Most certainly." Cordelia stifled a yawn.

"Here we are, ladies." The carriage came to a stop. Jake stepped out and offered his hand to help them down from the compartment.

"My, this is beautiful." Cordelia clasped a hand over her heart.

"Welcome to the O'Connor stables," Jake said with pride.

Chancy stepped out of the carriage and was awestruck. Miles of lush green grasses, white picket fences, and grazing horses of all colors surrounded her. "I think I'm in heaven," she stated awestruck by her surroundings.

Jake let out a chuckle. "This is only the beginning," he said, his voice full of pride. "Follow me, ladies. Simon, go ahead and park the carriage. I'll call for you later when the ladies are ready to return home."

The carriage driver, Simon, snapped the reins, the horses pulling the carriage moved forward. Jake placed a hand on Chancy's back and ushered her and her cousins, toward the two story building that served as a stable.

"This place is magnificent." Chancy looked around in wide eyed amazement.

"Wait until you see the inside," Jake boasted.

Chancy had never seen such riches. There were rows of stalls. Each was filled with fresh straw, the horses that occupied the area content as they strolled by.

"I'm getting mighty tired, Jake, do you by chance have an area where we could sit and rest?" Cordelia asked.

Chancy could see the bored expressions on her family's faces. They were doing their job well as escorts, but the horse talk was wearing them down.

"Yes, you ladies can rest in my office. I'll have someone

bring tea and refreshments. Chancy, I apologize if I've tired you and your family."

"Oh no, I'm fine. I'd love to have a look at your stallions. That is, if you don't mind showing me."

Mary sighed behind her. "Mary, Cordelia, Nettie, I'll be fine with Jake, if you all want to rest.
He's a perfect gentleman." Chancy glanced at Jake for reassurance.

"I'll keep your cousin in my strict care." Jake turned and smiled at her cousins.

"I'm sure you will," Nettie spoke up. "Come Mary, Cordelia, let's go have some tea while Chancy finishes looking at these horses."

Jake took her arm into the crook of his own. Chancy's stomach fluttered at the thought of being alone with him. But, she'd not pass on the chance to observe all his beautiful horseflesh. Together, they walked down the cobbled entryway. Jake stood a whole head taller than she, and when she turned to gaze at him, she was met by his intense, dark stare.

"What do you think so far?" he asked.

"I'm in love with this place." Chancy glanced around. A few paces ahead of them, a groom walked a sleek, dark bay horse into the aisle.

"Ahead is, Firewalker, my top stallion," Jake said with pride.

Chancy broke from his grasp and moved toward the horse. The horse's withers where above her head, the steed was so tall. She ran her hands down his shoulder and Firewalker brushed her arm with his muzzle.

"I've never seen anything like him." Chancy was in awe.

"Up ahead is one of his foals. Let's go take a look."

Together, they strolled four stalls down the walkway. Horses of varying colors poked their heads from their stalls and watched them as they walked by.

"This little one holds my future. I've named her Eponia." Jake stopped before the stall. Inside, a mother and her baby stared at them. The filly, curious, stepped forward and poked its small muzzle over the stall door.

Chancy giggled. "Oh my." She reached over and stroked the baby's soft face.

"Look at this little filly. She's long and lean—built to run. And her color...I've never seen a horse of this color." The filly had dark smoky coloring.

"I must say, Jake, you have a wonderful thing here." Chancy turned from the stall and looked at the man before her. His dark eyes glittered with pride. He took a step closer to her, his gaze intense.

Chancy's breath caught in her chest with his sudden move. She fidgeted with her dress, feelings of uncertainty plagued her. She liked Jake, shared his interest in horses, but the way he gazed at her made her uncertain of herself and of his intentions. She couldn't deny she enjoyed the attentions Jake had given her. But her true interest was in the horses. Jake, she'd never see again after today.

"I should get back. Cordelia and Mary will be ready to return home. I suppose I've broken more than enough rules of your society. I better get back, so not to cause any more scandal."

"As you wish, Chancy. It's been a joy having you here." Jake smiled down at her and reached for her arm once more then escorted her back to his office where her cousins and Nettie waited.

Chancy's mind was full of images from her day at the O'Connor stables. What a fine establishment he owned. Someday, the Mallory Ranch should be just as grand.

"Chancy, I think Jake is in love with you!" Mary squealed with delight on their way back to her cousins' home.

Chancy paled. "Mary, we share a common interest in horses. That's all."

Jake didn't accompany them on their return ride, to Chancy's relief. She'd have to have been blind not to notice there was something between them. Some kind of spark that made her heart flutter when she was around him. But it was over now, she'd never see Jake O' Connor again. She and her mother were to leave in the morning.

***

Chancy adjusted her simple brown traveling dress about her hips. Her bags had been packed the day before, she'd made sure she would be ready to leave this morning without a moment's delay. All that was left was to join her mother, aunt and cousins, for one last breakfast, then they'd be on their way home.

In her opinion the trip was a waste, she'd have been so much more useful this time of year back at the ranch, but her father had insisted she go with her mother on this journey. And she had met Jake and taken the opportunity to see some of the best racehorses in the state. That—she didn't regret.

Now, she knew what city living was like, of being a proper lady, and going to a ball for social enlightenment. All things she could do without and not even bat an eye. Breakfast conversation was filled with comments and excitement over the ball and of their outing to the O'Connor stables.

"Chancy, Jake O'Connor is quite smitten with you. He called you the prettiest western flower to grace the state of Nebraska!" Cordelia rattled on, "he's considered one of Omaha's best, most prestigious catches right now. Why, with his dark looks, and handsome smile, I bet he stole your heart away."

Chancy choked on her water. Her eyes watered when she looked at her cousins.

"Almost, but not quite," she answered. She smiled at their shocked expressions. They hadn't expected her to say this, and it made her happy that she was still the same Chancy Mallory she'd always been. City living wouldn't change who she was. Nor would it ever.

Yes, Jake was quite wonderful: strong, smart, even dangerous in an attractive way. She wouldn't deny enjoying her time in his arms on the dance floor, or at his stables, but a suitor right now wouldn't fit into her plans for the future. *But what about Nick?* Thoughts of him were always in the back of her mind.

Chancy and her mother said their farewells and headed for the front door. The buggy waited for them outside. Jim followed with their baggage. A loud rap was heard at the door. Jim set the travel cases down and proceeded to answer the door. An older man with a balding head, dressed in a brown overcoat, holding a letter stood at attention. Jim took the memo from the man then faced the ladies.

"Mrs. Mallory, it is addressed to, Miss Charlotte Mallory."

Chancy's heart hammered against her breastbone. *For me? Who would send me a note?*

"I bet the letter's from Jake." Cordelia squealed with delight, grasping Chancy's shoulder.

Chancy took the note and walked into the adjoining room. She needed a moment of privacy. Indeed, it was a short note in crisp black ink from the famous rogue, Jake O'Connor. The note was simple, telling her he'd enjoyed her company the previous day and hoped she'd visit Omaha again in the future. If she did, he'd like the privilege of escorting her to one of the actual horse races. The note made her breathless. A handsome man likes me. Picked me from all the glamorous beauties of the other night.

How can this be? Chancy was mystified.

When Chancy told her family, Mary and Cordelia couldn't contain their delight. "That young mans a brazen one," Chancy's Aunt Bethany spoke, a stern expression across her features.

"I've heard Jake O'Connor can be a bit of a rake and now he's proved to me it's true. I'm sorry for this slight on your honor, Chancy. I'll send word to reprimand Mr. O'Connor.

"No, Aunt Bethany it's really not necessary. I'll never see him again, and he was a perfect gentleman at the ball and while we were at the stables yesterday. Let's not make a huge fuss." No further discussion was brought forth regarding Jake O'Connor to Chancy's great relief and before she knew it she and her mother were back on the hard, cold seats of the train, on the tracks headed for home. Jake O'Connor's dangerous good looks a memory of the past.

CHAPTER TEN

Nick leaned against the barn entrance, Bones, nipped playfully at his heels while he watched Chancy's arrival to the ranch. He couldn't see her face from the distance, but by her animated hurried movements into the house he expected she'd be in a rush to change into her riding clothes and visit Bowie.

He'd brushed the mare until she gleamed this afternoon, and Bones too. The dog hadn't known how to react with the wiry comb across his back. He barked and growled and jumped around Nick's feet with the new game his master devised to play with him.

Nick's pulse raced with the thought of being near Chancy again. Time had escaped them with her absence, and already summer was in full swing. It was time to capture her colt, so she could prove to her father she was worthy of running this ranch.

Nick saddled two horses, one for himself, a spirited young mare he was working this week for one of the other hands and Bowie for Chancy. He expected she'd be in the barn for her evening ride soon, if her parents permitted it.

He heard footsteps in the distance, and Bones gave a bark of warning behind him. Chancy had arrived.

"A puppy, oh my goodness."

Nick turned to the sound of Chancy's voice. Chancy knelt to the ground. Bones happily jumped into her lap, a quick swish of his tongue across her cheek. The sound of her laughter melted his heart while Bones licked her face with relish.

"I love him, Nick. Where did you find him?" A wide smile covered Chancy's now wet face, covered in doggy slobbers.

"Found him in this barn one night, scared and hungry. We think his ma died out on the south side of the ranch."

"Oh, how terrible." The pup barked his agreement and

wagged his tail, his attention directed at Chancy.

"Ready to ride?" Nick asked, anxious to be on their way. Anna sometimes visited at this time of day. He didn't want to share Chancy with her just yet. He stepped forward and handed Chancy the reins to Bowie.

"Bowie sure looks good. Thanks for taking care of her for me while I was away." Chancy continued to talk, and he found he enjoyed her conversation. Anna on the other hand ground into his nerves as of late. He'd about had his fill of her nonstop talk. Only, he didn't know how to break it to her gently that he wasn't interested. The recent church social they had attended together was a nightmare.

"You don't know how long I've waited to get back here and do this once again. The city is so dark, full of strange smells, strange people. Oh Nick, the stories I have to tell."

Nick laughed at the expression on her face. Her features were alight and vivid with life. A sharp pang hit his chest, he hadn't realized how much he missed her until this moment.

Chancy mounted her horse and waited for him to do the same. Bones jumped around his legs while he checked his cinch one last time before pulling himself into the saddle.

"Where'd you come up with a name like that?" she asked. She squinted against the glare of the late afternoon sun while watching the puppy frolic about their horse's feet.

"I don't know, it just came to me and seemed to stick. When I first found him, the poor guy was just a bag of bones." Nick smiled and nudged his horse into a trot, leaving her behind him.

They loped across the pasture until the ranch disappeared into the distance. The air was cool and fresh on the plains. The young mare Nick rode bucked a few paces and then snorted and pawed the earth.

"Easy, girl. What's got you all worked up?"

"Quick—look up ahead. The mustangs!"

Chancy's excitement flowed to him and his heart beat faster with the appearance of the wild horses. They were running across the meadow in the distance, tails in the air, heads held high.

"Let's follow them."

Together, they spurred their horses into a gallop, Bones close at their heels. They followed the band for a short time before reining in. The stallion had turned and now faced them. A rebellious snort reverberated from his nostrils.

"He's getting touchy with us so close to his mares. We better back off a bit before he charges."

Nick halted his horse and Chancy followed suit.

"I think we should try to bring Snowbar in tomorrow. The sooner we start to work with him the better. Soon, he'll be pushed away by this big guy, and he and his pals will be off on their own adventures."

Nick glanced over at Chancy, a look of horror crossed her face. He knew a lot was riding on her capturing and taming this horse. "You're still are up for this, aren't you?"

Chancy stared at Nick, the words he'd spoken had terrified her. She had to capture Snowbar. He was her ace in the hole. Proof to her father she was more than just a well defined young lady of the house.

Since her return this afternoon, the walls of the ranch had moved in on her. On the way home, her mother had talked on and on about the joys of living in the city, how it would benefit Chancy for the future. The charming boy who'd shared a few dances with her. With each word her mother spoke, Chancy had become more and more fearful for her future and what her parents may have planned. Icy tentacles of fear gripped her heart.

"Tomorrow it is," she spoke with finality. Let's ride to the hole and make our plans. Chancy reached the corralled space first and dismounted, letting Bowie drink from the stream while she looked around. Much needed doing, but they'd only hours to complete the tasks.

"Where do we start?" Chancy stared at Nick who had dismounted behind her. Bones wandered about, sniffing at the plants and trees. A jackrabbit ran out from under a cluster of sagebrush and he ran off in pursuit.

"Well, let's first make sure the corral will hold him when we run him through here tomorrow. Let's start at this end and work our way around." Not waiting for further instruction, Chancy tied her horse to a tree and paced the wooden enclosure.

Together, they mended the broken areas of the fence. Mostly in silence, they were short on time and had too much work to do to talk. When the sun crested over the mountain, it was time to return to the ranch.

"We better head back, your folks will wonder what we're up to." Nick wiped a bead of sweat from his forehead, leaving a dusty smudge behind.

"We're so close, just the south end is left to check. I'll try to get out here after my chores and get started until you can make it out here tomorrow."

Chancy wasn't afraid to do this on her own. In fact, before she and Nick had made a truce, she'd planned on capturing the colt by herself anyhow. Nick's help had been much appreciated, and she knew without it, she may never succeed.

Bone tired and weary, Chancy took Bowie's reins and mounted. Nick was already mounted and waiting. "Bones," he called. The pup ran out of the tall grass near the stream upon hearing his name. "It's good to have you back, Chancy." Nick smiled at her, before spurring his horse into a trot toward the ranch.

***

"You go on inside, and I'll take care of the horses." Nick stopped his horse and dismounted when they'd reached the barn.

Tired as she was, Chancy found it hard to argue tonight. For once she agreed to let Nick help her with her responsibility.

"All right." She handed the reins to her friend and then leaned down to pet Bones on the top of the head.

"Nick, there you are, I wondered where you'd disappeared tonight." Anna walked over and put her arm around his waist.

"Hi, Chancy, my mother said you'd returned. How was your trip?"

Chancy paused at the sound of Anna's voice and turned toward Nick. His gaze was locked into hers.

"It was nice, Anna. How has your time been?"

"Well, did Nick tell you about the church social? We went together. It was so wonderful."

Chancy noted Anna laid her head against Nick's shoulder. Nick's face was pensive and withdrawn. Something weird was going on.

"Thanks again..." She couldn't think of anything else to say. Nick stepped forward and reached for her hand. His was warm and rough in her own. The contact sent ripples of excitement clear to her toes. He squeezed lightly and then let her hand drop once more. The loss sent a cold chill over her heart.

"Any time," he answered.

Chancy made her way toward the ranch house.

"Chancy—wait for me," Anna called out and ran to catch up with her.

"Isn't Nick just the best. Can you believe he kissed me? Oh Chancy, he is the best kisser in the world. I think I'm in love."

Chancy's stomach churned. She swallowed the nausea threatening to rise in her throat. What did she expect? Anna was the beauty here, Nick would be crazy not to fall for her. Chancy blinked back tears. *I'm just tired.* Tomorrow's a new day, and I have a colt to catch.

CHAPTER ELEVEN

Chancy woke before the rooster could crow the next morning. The stars were crisp in the fading night sky, not a cloud could be seen and the glow of the moon cast a shimmery iridescence over the horses corralled next to the barn.

She squinted her eyes against the windowpane. A lone cowboy waded through the horses, lasso in hand. He twirled the rope and snagged an unsuspecting horse. The mount fought for a moment.

Chancy imagined the whites of horse's eyes showing as it tugged against the rope. The mount quickly gave in and calmed.

Nick, who else would walk up to the horse and rub its neck and shoulder to sooth it before leading it to the barn. He had a kind and gentle heart toward animals. Bones was proof of his compassion.

Most of the other hands would have sent the little pup on his way, taken him to town to find him a home. Chancy was finding it harder and harder not to like Nick Stone. *But he's fallen for Anna.* Anna's words of the night before came back to haunt her. Nick had kissed her. *You need to get the colt, not worry about what Nick does,* she reminded herself. The thought stung anyhow.

The day's chores went smooth, much to Chancy's delight. Her mother had gone to a neighboring ranch to visit, and Chancy had the house to herself. She cleaned and dusted and prepped the food for the night's dinner. Chores complete, she rushed upstairs to change into her riding clothes.

With no one around to reprimand her, she ran to the barn. The wind felt good blowing through her hair, the air was warm and scented with fresh hay the men had put into the barn the last few days.

She breathed deep enjoying the heavy fragrance. Minutes

later, Bowie was saddled and ready. Chancy mounted and kicked the horse into a run.

Her heart thundered against her breastbone with what she had planned for today. Her future depended on the outcome, but with Nick's help she knew she would succeed.

As the hidden corral drew near she pulled Bowie into a steady trot. The mustangs were nowhere in sight, but she knew they wouldn't stray far. The best grazing was in this stretch of land. That was why her father always allowed the men to capture the mustangs this time of year, it was easy as netting spawning fish. Dip in the net and pull up the fish, chase the horses into the chute and they were contained in the corral. She hoped.

After Bowie was secured to a tree branch, Chancy finished walking the last stretch of corral they'd been unable to check yesterday. The corral was secure from what Chancy could see. Butterflies fluttered in her stomach. It was time.

Pulling her hat low over her forehead, lariat in hand, Chancy scanned the horizon. She spurred Bowie into a ground eating gallop. Leaning low over her horse's mane, she followed fresh tracks leading to the flower filled bowl which consisted of Wild Horse Lake, a huge watering hole for the wild animals in the mountain ranges. Her hunch was correct; ahead the herd grazed among the meadow grasses, next to the beautiful lake.

Chancy scanned the area for her colt. He was off to the side of the herd, with several other young colts. Nick was right, it would be a matter of days before the stallion shooed the colt and his friends from the rest of the herd.

She circled wide and loosened the lariat in her hand. Moving Bowie to the inside her hope was to circle the colts and send them running toward the corral. She spurred her horse, and they were off covering the sometimes rocky uneven ground at a steady pace.

Her plan was working, the horses were moving the direction she desired. Her eyes watered and her vision blurred with the pace she'd set. She trusted Bowie's footing on this terrain and held tight when her horseshoe slid on an occasional rock.

A fine lather built on her mount's sides, perspiration covered her forehead and dampness caused her shirt to stick to her back. She kept the horses moving up over the bluff with a slap of her rope against her thigh. She was close to reaching the enclosure.

"Keep em coming!" She could hear Nick's voice in the backdrop. Not daring a glance back she pressed on.

"We're close!" Nick whooped. With a rush, the mustangs ran into the pen, Chancy beside them.

"We've done it!" Nick's cry of triumph sent a thrill up her spine.

Chancy pulled Bowie to a halt, the horse slid on her hocks before she stopped and turned on her haunches to face Nick. A wide grin graced his features and his blue eyes gleamed with pride.

"Chancy, you're something else. You were pretty close to having those mustangs rounded up in here on your own. I'm plum amazed!"

She couldn't help but return his smile. She wiped the beads of sweat from her brow, removing her hat and dusting it off against her knee. She gave Bowie a pat on the shoulder.

"All in a day's work for a rancher." She laughed.

"You'll make a fine rancher, Chancy, don't let anyone tell you any different."

The look on his face said he meant what he said. It meant a lot to her that he was on her side.

"When can we start working him?" She glanced over at the spotted colt while he and the others ran up and down the corral bumping into the fence as they searched for a weakened area to escape.

Mustangs, she knew from experience, were cunning creatures.

"I think tomorrow should be soon enough. It's getting late; we don't want anyone from the ranch to get suspicious. We'll meet here tomorrow afternoon and start. Before we leave, let's get these stragglers out before the stallion tries to break them all free. I'll keep the colt cornered while you run those others out."

They worked as a team and before long, the colt was by himself inside the enclosure.

"I think Bowie deserves a good rubdown for her work today, huh girl?" Chancy rubbed the horse's shoulder now dried with sweat. The afternoon went by faster than Chancy would have liked.

Before she knew it she was back inside the ranch house staring down her parents while they waited for her at the dinner table.

"What have you been up to the last several evenings?" Chancy's father asked, between sips of his coffee. Her mother sat in the chair nearest her father and stared at her expectantly.

Chancy cleared her throat, the fear that always clutched at her heart when talk of her and the ranch came up caught her off guard.

"I rode out on the ranch with Nick. Bowie's out of shape from not being ridden while I was away," she offered.

Her father's eyebrows raised at her explanation. He tweaked his mustache before setting his coffee cup on the table.

"I was hoping you'd be more involved in domestic pursuits with your return from Omaha. Chancy, at some point you're going to have to let go of your barn chores and start behaving like a lady."

Chancy wondered if she'd swallowed a rock. Her tongue was thick. She ground her teeth together, the aftertaste worse than if her mouth was filled with sand. Her words were caught in her throat and her eyes burned.

"Jim, give her some time. There's always a transition from being a wild tomboy to a proper lady. She did a wonderful job of acting genteel while we were in Omaha. I couldn't be more proud."

"May I be excused?" No longer hungry and feeling a little faint, all Chancy wanted was to escape to her room. Out of earshot from her parents.

"Yes, dear. That'll be fine," her mother answered after a few moments.

Once in her room, Chancy gave into her tears. She'd completed all her *domestic* chores today as her father liked to call them. Was that not good enough? She lay on her bed and wept until she was too exhausted to cry anymore. *Will pa ever understand?* This was a question that never strayed far from the back of her mind.

When the house was quiet except for the creaks and moans of the old floorboards, Chancy made her escape to the barn. She tiptoed down the hallway and down the stairs. Step by step, she made her way to the door. With a creak it opened, and she stepped outside with a breath of relief.

She then ran down the dirt road to the barn and opened the doors to step inside. There, the soft snorts of horses calmed her. She moved toward Bowie's stall and opened the latch to step inside.

Before she could, Bones was at her feet.

"What are you doing in here, boy?" She knelt down and pulled the puppy to her chest. He licked her with excitement. His soft brown eyes full of trust. *Strange,* where's Nick? She wondered. The barn was quiet and dark, she sat still and listened for movement, but there was none other than the horses and Bones.

"Where's Nick, boy, did he leave you in here all alone?" She stroked the top of the pup's head then stood again and stepped inside Bowie's stall. The horse's soft muzzle met her, and she rubbed her face against the horse's silky cheek.

"Oh, girl, I don't know what I'll do if pa say's I can't ride anymore." Tears formed once again in the corners of her eyes as she hugged the horse's neck. Bowie was her best friend in the world. It broke her heart knowing her father may not allow her to ride anymore.

Nick listened from the distance. He'd come to the barn, unable to sleep. Guilt for all his actions as of late kept him awake. The sound of snores kept him and Bones awake, then the pup wanted to play.

So, they'd trekked to the barn so Nick could check on the horses and his tack for tomorrow and let Bones wear himself out. He'd been surprised when he'd heard the soft footsteps of Chancy enter the barn.

Should he show himself and explain to Chancy about Anna? Tell Chancy he thought of Anna as only a friend and nothing more? Then thoughts of how he'd left his parents came back to haunt him. He wondered how his family fared. He'd sent a letter to them when he first arrived at the Mallory ranch, but had not heard back from them as of yet.

With the thought of confronting Chancy, he froze in place. The words he'd heard her say shook him to the core. Her tears tore at him, and he wanted nothing more than to take her in his arms and comfort her. That would be impossible. Instead. he hid in the shadows, fists clinched and listened to her speak to Bowie in whispers of her sorrows.

When she left, Nick sighed a breath of relief. The muscles in his neck were tense, and he knew sleep would elude him this night. He walked to the nearest stall and stroked a soft muzzle. The pile of hay in the corner of the barn beckoned him. It wouldn't be the first time he'd found comfort and solace in the barn with the horses, instead of his bed.

CHAPTER TWELVE

"First thing I want you to do is follow Snowbar around while on Bowie. Stay close, but not in his space. Let him get used to seeing you and having you near."

Chancy nodded and nudged Bowie forward. Today was an important day, the first step in Snowbar's training. Ignoring the sweat which burned her eyes, she remained side by side to the beautiful colt. She'd never been this close to him before now.

His hide was a silvery white with large black spots of varying shapes and sizes over his body. His mane and tail were a pale shade of silver and glistened in the sunlight. Snowbar was a befitting name, for he glistened like the snow on a sunny day.

Nick hung back atop his horse, while she followed the colt. She was gaining his trust, minute by minute. The colt started to relax, head lowered and jaws moving, he no longer was in flight mode.

Snowbar settled into a slow but steady pace, keeping his ears pointed in her direction while he watched her every move. Nick's method was working.

"Let's call it a day. Let him rest, and he'll be ready for us tomorrow." Nick waved at her when she turned in the saddle to the sound of his voice.

She reined Bowie around and rode to where he waited for her. Excitement lined his face and her hopes soared.

"How do you think I did?" she asked, worried she may have made some blunder along the way.

"Perfect. Snowbar's a smart boy, and he'll be eating out of your palm in the next day or so, you just wait."

Nick's words eased her mind. They fell into a comfortable silence while watching Snowbar start to graze.

"There's something I've wanted to talk to you about, Chancy."

Startled, she glanced his way. "You don't want to help me?" Her blood turned to ice in her veins. She needed his help in this. He couldn't walk away now.

"No, not that. It's about Anna." His gaze fell to the ground and he fiddled with his horse's reins.

Chancy noticed the discomfort written across his features. She'd dreaded this conversation for days. Whatever Nick needed to say couldn't be good. Especially, since she had feelings for him herself.

"Nick, you really don't need to explain anything to me. Anna thinks she's in love with you. And how could anyone not fall for her? She's pretty, smart, good in the kitchen... I won't intrude upon your relationship. I just need your help with Snowbar, then, I promise not to bother you again."

Nick groaned aloud. "Chancy, listen to me. I do not *love* Anna. When she mentioned I kissed her the other day, I admit, I did. On the cheek. A friendly peck after the church social. That was all. I do not love her."

A great relief washed through her then. Hope rose from the pit of her stomach. "Okay then, I believe you." She couldn't keep the smile off her face. Nick remained quiet, his gaze fixed on her. He opened his mouth to speak, then quickly clamped his lips tight. Chancy noted his face was twisted in a befuddled look.

"Let's meet here tomorrow." He finally spoke before he rode away.

***

The next day, Chancy followed the same regime. She shadowed the colt's every move, until he no longer feared her nearness. The colt followed her, his ears pointed wherever she went, and when he'd lower his head, she'd back off the pressure to give him room so he could decide his next move.

This went on for several hours, until Snowbar no longer feared their presence. By the end of the session, Chancy could ride up to the colt. He stood rigid and his ears pricked forward, but inch by inch she reached over and lay her hand on his silky hide. He felt like heaven under her touch, his coat was softer than spun silk. When she looked up and into Nick's eyes, the excitement and approval she noted there sent a rush of emotion through her. In that split second she realized over the last few months something had changed in how she felt about him. A strong bond had been formed these lasts weeks, and she knew when Nick was near her life felt complete.

***

"All right this is it, are you ready?" Nick's expression was serious as he held the lead to Snowbar. Chancy took a deep breath to gather her courage. They'd worked with the colt all week and so far all had gone well. Nick had saddled the colt yesterday and Snowbar had taken to the saddle and bridle with trust.

Today, Chancy was going to get on Snowbar's back for the first time. Nick had talked her through what she needed to do and how to act and react with each movement of the horse. She'd listened to him with rapt attention all the while studying his features.

His eyes had always caught her attention, the intense crisp blue that they were. He had broad shoulders and stood tall and straight, confidence seeped from him to those around him. He was quiet, but kind and courteous. Traits Chancy loved about him.

When she'd been back East and her cousins had hounded her about if she'd ever been kissed, Chancy hadn't given the idea a second thought. Now, since her return, it was all she could think of.

Each time they were together, Chancy found herself studying his mouth and wondered what it might be like to have his lips touch hers. But then thoughts of Anna crept into her mind. Anna told her she was in love with Nick. *But wasn't she in love every other week?* Didn't Nick tell her he didn't share those feelings with her friend? All the thoughts jumbled around in her head until it ached.

"Chancy, did you hear me?"

She turned at the sound of his voice. Nick's features were strained. His expression full of unspoken questions.

"Sorry, yes—I'm ready." She needed to focus. Without a second thought, she put her foot into the stirrup and watched the colt for a response. He stood still, ears pricked forward and alert but showed no resistance. Satisfied, Chancy pulled herself up and over the saddle. The colt remained frozen beneath her. Slowly, she lowered her backside into the saddle.

"Easy now, Chancy, he's doing good. Talk to him quiet, tell him he's a good boy."

Chancy followed Nick's instruction, she reached forward and stroked the horse's shoulder. The colt's muscles trembled under her touch. "Good boy," she cooed to soothe him.

Moments later, the colt took a hesitant step forward. Chancy relaxed in the saddle and the colt walked out. She continued to speak in quiet tones while they made their way around the enclosure.

"I can't believe I'm doing this. I'm actually riding Snowbar." Chancy couldn't contain her excitement.

"He's a fast learner, and he trusts you. He'll make you a good ranch horse. He's built solid, and we know from watching him out on the range he's got speed. You made a good pick, Chancy."

Nick smiled at her from the ground. At that moment Chancy believed if there was such a thing as soul mates then surely Nick must be hers.

"Let's call this a day. We'll do a bit more riding tomorrow. We've made a lot of progress this week. Another two weeks, and you should be able to ride him to the ranch. Show your pa what you've accomplished.

Chancy dismounted. She ran her hands along Snowbar's neck and shoulder then rubbed

between his eyes. He nudged her with his muzzle and made her laugh. "Silly boy, what do you think you need? A treat?" Chancy pulled a sugar cube from her pocket. The colt took the offering from her palm and chewed it with relish.

"He's a beauty isn't he?"

Nick's warm breath tickled the back of her neck. A chill of excitement shot down her spine with the intimacy. *Should I risk it?* Before she could talk herself out of what her heart desired, she turned and in one movement covered his lips with her own.

The kiss was quick, but sent a jolt of exhilaration clear to her toes. Her stomach fluttered with the passion from it. When she opened her eyes, Nick's gaze held a shocked and amused expression.

"Chancy," his words came out little more than a whisper.

"Sorry, I shouldn't have." Chancy ducked her head. A heated flush rose up her neck to cover her cheeks.

Nick's hand warmed her shoulder. "Chancy?"

Chancy raised her chin and dared a glance into his eyes. He leaned forward, head tilted until their lips touched once more. Little sparks of delight ran through her veins. Nick deepened the kiss and time, Chancy was sure, stood still.

His lips were soft, and she yielded to his demands. His tongue explored the inner recesses of her mouth. He tasted of an exotic mixture of mint and something purely Nick. He pulled her against his chest until their hearts beat as one.

When Nick stepped back, Chancy had never felt so breathless. She was speechless, her mind still lost in the kiss.

"Chancy, I was out of place. I didn't mean to take things this far."

His words stung worse than a hornet bite she'd had last summer. She didn't want him to be sorry. She wanted him to tell her she was his and his only. But the words she hoped for never came.

CHAPTER THIRTEEN

Nick didn't regret the kiss. In fact, he'd hoped for the chance to do just that for some time. When Chancy made the first move his heart was set in motion. She appeared a little abashed, but she was strong willed, she'd have never have done something if she hadn't meant it. Things had changed between them since her return from Omaha. They'd forged a strong bond between them.

"Want to ride to the lake before we return to the ranch?" Chancy's question had caught him off guard again. He'd expected that she'd want to stay away from him, take time to explore her feelings. He knew he needed to. From here on out things would forever be changed between them.

"Okay, let's go," he replied. Her cheek was covered in a streak of sweat and dust. He leaned over and wiped her face with his hand. Her skin was soft under his touch. He saw her swallow, her gaze intense, while she watched him.

They left Snowbar secured in the enclosure and rode toward Wild Horse Lake. One of the many lakes which graced these lands. The water was spring fed from underground springs and glacier runoff throughout the year. The meadows that surrounded the body of water were still filled with grass and wildflowers of various colors. Nick leaned over to pick an orange paintbrush. He would give it to Chancy later.

They rode to the lake in silence. A comfortable, calm type of quiet. A golden eagle soared overhead. Nick always experienced peace when he and Chancy had these hours alone. Guilt once again gnawed at his insides. How long would this last? He hadn't planned on remaining at the Mallory ranch forever. Just one of the many stops he'd make while searching out his own piece of heaven. He pushed those thoughts to the side.

He'd stay a short time longer, if only for the chance to be near Chancy.

***

The water was cool against his skin. He'd removed his shirt and dove head first into the clear blue waters of the lake. Its frigid temperature cooled him at once. Goosebumps rose on his forearms as he stood up, the rocky bottom of the lake tickling his feet.

"Are you going to get in?" he called to Chancy, who watched from the sandy shore. When she shook her head, he splashed water in her direction.

"Hey," she called out. The front of her shirt was now wet, and water dripped off the end of her nose.

"That's not fair. You know I can't get in with you. It would be...well—improper." She eyed him with suspicion.

Of course, she was right. If her father, or one of the other hands rode by, his job and reputation would be on the line, not to mention Chancy's honor. She was old enough for marriage, and her parents letting her ride without an escort of the female kind would be shocking to some. He needed to maintain his good sense and protect her.

"All right, I'll let you off easy this time," he chanted before splashing water in her direction once more and ducking under the waters depths.

Refreshed, he emerged from the lake, droplets of water running down his bare chest. He walked to where Chancy sat at the edge of the bank, her feet devoid of boots, soaking in the water.

Nick sat beside her and leaned back on his elbows. The warmth of the afternoon sun dried him and the sun's rays made him drowsy.

"What do you think your pa will say when you ride Snowbar onto the ranch?" Nick asked.

Chancy remained quiet. She stared into the distance for some time before she answered.

"I'm not sure, but I hope he believes me when I say I want

to carry on the legacy of this ranch.

That's all I can hope for." Chancy lay back on the grass and stared into the sky. "Ever wish you could be something you're not?" She asked out of the blue.

"No...Well—maybe," he answered, confused. He lay back next to her. Chancy tilted her head in his direction. Her eyes were rimmed with a touch of sadness when she looked at him. He gave her a small smile and took her hand in his own, entwining his fingers through hers.

"I heard something once you might like. It's kind of silly, but... if anyone would understand, I think it would be you." A hint of warmth spread across his cheeks.

"Well—go on, you have my curiosity peaked now." Chancy gave his hand a light squeeze.

Suddenly, he felt silly for mentioning such a thing. Poetry was not something he ever thought he'd admit to knowing. Chancy seemed to bring out a side of him he wasn't familiar with.

"Okay—but don't laugh."

"I won't laugh—I promise." Chancy smiled at him.

"Here it goes." He cleared his throat before he began. "With flowing tail and flying mane, Wide nostrils, never stretched by pain, Mouth bloodless to bit or rein, And feet that iron never shod, And flanks unscar'd by spur or rod A thousand horses - the wild - the free - Like waves that follow o'er the sea, Came thickly thundering on."

"Oh, Nick—that's the most beautiful thing I've ever heard." Nick saw tears glittered in her eyes.

She moved closer to him, until their noses almost touched. He closed his eyes and breathed in her scent. Wildflowers, fresh air, horses. That was Chancy. A scent he'd never tire of. The world between them stilled in this moment. He opened his eyes once more, to see hers were wide, full of passion. He wanted to kiss her again, ached for the contact with her as he stared into her face, but in the end pulled back.

"Thanks, I didn't make it up. The poem was actually written by a poet named Lord Byron. It's just something I read in the past and it stuck in my brain."

"It's wonderful." Chancy lay back again. He could hear the disappointment in her tone. She wanted him to kiss her again, had seen the hunger in her eyes, but instead he withdrew. *What am I doing?* He should kick himself for getting her hopes up. This wasn't his home or where he planned to stay. He was a drifter trying to find his own way in the world.

"We better get back to the ranch." Nick stood and helped Chancy to her feet. She brushed by him and grabbed the reins to Bowie without another word.

The ride back to the ranch was short, Chancy kept Bowie at a steady lope, Nick hung behind. *She needs her space,* he reasoned. At the barn she went through her chores in a quick and efficient manner. To make matters worse, Anna arrived at the barn to talk to him.

Now was the time to put a stop to her fanciful thoughts, he reasoned. "Anna, we need to talk, there's something I need to tell you."

"Well, let's take a walk then shall we?" She grabbed his arm and pulled him out of the barn.

"Chancy must be fit to be tied about something. She wouldn't even speak to me when I came into the barn." Anna sniffed. "Ever since she came back from the city, she will hardly speak to me. If I didn't know better, I'd think she's become a little stuck up."

Flabbergasted, Nick stopped in his tracks. He wasn't going to listen to Anna complain about Chancy all afternoon. "Anna, you need to stop telling folks we're a couple. I like you as a friend, but that's all."

"But you took me out horseback riding—and the walks? I thought we were a couple. How about the church social?" She pouted.

Nick couldn't believe his ears. He'd done all those things out of friendship, and somehow she'd twisted it around in her mind to mean something else. "Anna, we're just friends, nothing more," he stated matter of fact." He watched a rainbow of emotions cross her face. Anger, suspicion, then tears formed in her eyes.

"You know what, Nick Stone. You and Chancy deserve each other. You both think you're so high and mighty with all you know about horses." She stomped her foot. "I planned on moving on anyhow. Chancy can have you." Anna turned and stormed away. She stopped suddenly and turned toward him once more. A thoughtful expression came over her features and she smiled at him.

"Maybe I should tell you this. It will be for your own good. My mother told me when Chancy was in Omaha, her mother said all the boys were eating out of her hand. And, Chancy was invited to a prestigious stable by a rich young man by the name of Jake O'Connor." Anna stroked her chin, "I believe that was his name. Chancy's mother said he's rich beyond measure with a stable full of race horses. And her mother believes the boy was half in love with Chancy. Chew on that—Nick Stone." With those parting words she left in a rush, her dress swishing about her ankles.

Nick's heart dropped to his stomach. He didn't understand females one lick. Anna or Chancy. Chancy had never mentioned the race horses to him. Not that it was his business. And now she was just as miffed at him as Anna, but there was nothing he could do to change things with Chancy. "He's rich with his own stable full of horses..." Anna's words echoed in his mind. Their relationship was doomed before it ever began. It would be for the best to keep some distance from Chancy for things could never be between them.

***

Chancy was unable to sleep that night. The past months' memories kept her awake. From the moment she met Nick, to her trip to Omaha. Her first kiss, and Nick's romantic words. Her body still tingled from Nick's touch, and the hardness of his lips against her own. She wanted more. More kisses that stole her breath away.

Only, when she'd looked into his eyes at the lake, she'd caught the hooded expression which overcame his smile. He'd retreated from her, into some dark place she couldn't reach, he didn't want her to find.

Nick was the one, somehow she knew this clear to her bones. It didn't matter there had been no other boys in her life. None that she'd ever met in the past had lit her soul as he did. Not even the handsome Jake O'Connor. Now, she just needed to show Nick they were meant for each other.

The next morning, Chancy drank an extra cup of coffee before starting her daily routine. She was sluggish and morose. "Chancy, do you feel unwell?" her mother asked.

"I'm fine, Ma," she'd lied. It was a small white lie, but guilt still gnawed at her soul, for lying wasn't something she condoned. But she wouldn't risk having her barn chores taken away.

That afternoon, when she arrived at the barn, she noticed Nick was nowhere in sight. *He's avoiding me.* She didn't know if she should be angry or relieved. She went about her chores, cleaning Bowie's stall and brushing her fine coat. Still no Nick. "Well, we'll just go visit the colt on our own then, won't we girl?"

Chancy saddled her horse then after looking around the barn once more and still no Nick, she rode out on her own. When she reached Snowbar's enclosure, Nick wasn't there either. Where'd he go? she wondered. She swallowed the anger that threatened to ruin her afternoon.

She saddled Snowbar and put him through his paces, but it wasn't the same without Nick there at her side. And, if her father, or any of the men saw her working a wild mustang on her own, she'd be forever in trouble. So, disappointment a bitter taste in her mouth, she left the mustang and rode back to the ranch. There, she found Nick in one of the back stalls, shirt off, shoveling fresh straw into the pen.

The sight of him with no shirt, skin glistening, muscles rippling, took her breath away. She stood motionless, watching in awestruck fascination. When he turned toward her and then turned away, anger washed through her. How dare he?

"Where were you?" she asked, unable to keep the haughty tone at bay.

"I had other things to do today. Actually for the rest of the week. I'd suggest you give Snowbar a few days rest, until I can ride out with you again." Nick continued to work without looking at her.

"Why so busy all of a sudden?" she challenged.

"Chancy, I'm just a ranch hand here. I have responsibilities to your father—my boss."

His words stung. They were devoid of the emotion they'd shared yesterday. Chancy wracked her brain in an attempt to figure out what had caused this change. She put Bowie away without another word. She watched him out of the corner of her eye. Every so often, she caught him looking in her direction, a pained look on his face. Why was he putting distance between them now? Confused and hurt, Chancy left the barn without a goodbye.

Chancy tried to be merry at dinner with her parents. But their chatter only deepened her depression. "May I be excused?" she finally asked, unable to take their conversation any further.

"Yes—you may," her mother answered. Chancy pushed away from the table, ignoring the suspicious glances of her parents.

"Is everything okay, Chancy? You haven't been this distracted for some time."

"I'm fine, Ma, just tired is all. Goodnight everyone." Chancy left the room, the burn of her parents glances scorched her back. She didn't want to talk with her parents tonight. She wanted to crawl into bed and cry. Never had she been so distressed. And all for a boy. Her heart ached at the absence of Nick's laughter, his smiles. She had it bad, she didn't know when it happened, but somewhere along the way she'd fallen under his spell. And now he wanted to back away, act as if nothing had occurred between them.

Chancy scrambled into bed, covered her face with a pillow and let the tears stream down her face. She turned toward the window and stared at the moon. A soft breeze blew through the opening in the window. Chancy fell asleep to the sound of a lonesome coyote howling in the distance.

***

The rest of the week dragged on. Nick was away, her pa sent him to a line shack far from her reach. She missed his conversation and his company. Several days she'd rode out to Snowbar and worked him under saddle. He responded well, he trusted her, and she was able to put him through his paces with no troubles.

When Nick returned, she would ride Snowbar to the ranch and show her father what she'd been up to. If Nick still wished to help her. He'd acted so strange the last week, she wasn't sure where she stood with him.

That night dinner began as it always did, her father and mother sat at the table in light conversation. Their heads where drawn together, and she noticed deep furrows on her father's face.

Something was up. He only had that look when something was wrong. Chancy's heart beat a little faster against her ribcage. For some odd reason she wondered if tonight her life was going to change.

She sat at her place at the table and poured herself a glass of milk. Out of the corner of her eye she noticed her parents watched her in silence. "Is something wrong?" she asked, unable to contain her growing worry.

"Chancy." Her father cleared his throat.

When she glanced up, she noticed her mother's face had paled, and her father's held a pink hue, and he twirled his mustache with his index finger. Bad signs, she knew.

"One of the men saw you today," he began.

Chancy's stomach did a series of somersaults. She knew where this was going.

"They said you were riding one of the mustangs from the band. The silver coated Appaloosa. Is this true, Chancy?"

His face grew redder by the minute. Chancy knew she was

in deep trouble now.

"Pa, I can explain." She paused.

"Please do, young lady. What are you trying to do, kill yourself? I can't believe you'd do such a foolish thing. What if you'd been hurt, no one would have known where you were," her mother's voice wavered on the edge of hysteria.

"I warned you about riding out on the range without an escort of some kind. But you went against my wishes anyhow." Her father's voice shook with controlled anger.

Panic clenched at her heart. There was no denying any of the charges. She ducked her head prepared to take her punishment like an adult.

"Nick and I..."

"I knew it," her mother scoffed, "I told you Nick was behind this." Her mother stomped her foot on the floor.

"Alma, I trust Nick and his judgment with horses. I don't trust his judgment with my daughter's life. I'll have one of the men bring him in from the line shack, so I can talk with him."

"Pa, Nick didn't do anything wrong. It was all my idea, he only offered to help. Snowbar—he's an amazing horse. I was going to wait until Nick returned to ride him to the ranch, but since you now know..."

"Young lady, you'll be riding that mustang nowhere. Do you hear me?" her father's voice shook.

His gaze narrowed in on her and his face was clouded with anger.

"Chancy, we were going to wait to tell you, but I guess now is as good of time as any. Your Aunt Bethany and cousins have asked for your return to Omaha. You will be able to finish your studies there. You'll have exposure to culture and shopping and so much more than what we can give you here on the ranch."

Chancy was speechless. She knew whatever her parents had to say would be bad, but to send her away to Omaha, her voice was frozen and her heart, she was sure stopped beating.

"No..." she managed after a moment. "I won't go. I don't want to be exposed to culture. This ranch is where I belong—my life is here on the ranch. This is what I want. A chance to one day fill your shoes, Pa."

Her father's expression darkened. "Chancy, the ranch is made for a man's work. You do a wonderful job with the horses, but there's so much more. There're ranch hands to handle, cattle, horses to buy and sell. More than any girl or woman should have to worry about. I want you to have life with the things your mother and I were never able to give you. The culture in Omaha is a chance most girls your age would jump to take."

"I'm sorry, I can't do this." Unable to stand being in the same room with her parents a second longer, she rushed out and ran up the staircase to her room. Her door shut behind her with a loud thud.

Chancy threw herself on her bed. She was too upset to cry, instead her body shook, her stomach clinched and her pulse raced through her veins. No, no no, her mind screamed. Her worst nightmare was coming true. A knock at her door brought her up short.

"Chancy, may I come in?" her mother's words from behind the door seemed to lock in her fate.

There was more and it wouldn't be good.

"Sure," she called out.

Her mother strode into her room. Chancy raised her head and met her gaze head on.

"Chancy, your aunt sent a train ticket for your return. You'll leave at the end of the week."

"I have no choice in this?" Chancy asked on the verge of tears.

"Chancy, this is in your best interest. You can finish the last of your studies and be involved in all the functions young ladies your age attend. If you stay here, there will be nothing for you."

"Ma, that's not true. I love it here. This is my life. Why can't you and pa understand this?" The tears came then in a great torrent.

"Chancy, once you're back in Omaha, I think you'll learn

to enjoy yourself. I would have loved a chance for such an adventure when I was your age. Please try to understand, your pa and I are doing this in your best interest."

Chancy could tell by the set of her mother's chin there would be no further arguments. Her fate was sealed. She would be shipped back to Omaha to act the proper lady. She needed a plan and fast.

CHAPTER FOURTEEN

The night sky became a black shroud with the incoming storm. The ominous clouds fit her mood tonight. She stared out the windowpane and into the distance. Claps of thunder shook the glass in the window frame and lightening lit the backdrop of the sky. The air smelled acrid, and the slight breeze which blew into the room was warm and moist.

It's now or never, Chancy reasoned. She stepped away from the window and opened her bedroom door. She paused at the entrance and tilted her head to listen. Her parents room was at the far end of the hall. Escape would be easy. She needed to get to Nick. This was her focus, the rest, if he agreed would fall into place, once they were together.

Quiet as a mouse, Chancy tip-toed down the hallway. With each creak in the wooden floorboards she cringed, but did not stop. It wasn't unusual for the house to shift during the night with the frequent temperature changes, her parents should not be suspicious.

Once at the front door, she grabbed her duster and hat to keep dry. Then, without a glance behind her, she ran down the road toward the barn and Bowie. It would be a good few hours before she reached Nick, and with the onslaught of this storm, possibly longer.

The lightning flashed closer, and a chill ran down her spine. Riding in this weather was dangerous. But the ranch hands rode in these conditions often to protect the herds. Bowie, raised and trained on these lands wouldn't be spooked by the noise at least.

At the barn, she raced inside. The horses, dozing in the darkness, became alert with her arrival ears twitching, snorting their discontent. Several pawed their stalls, demanding attention. Chancy ignored their nickers and strode straight to Bowie's stall. The horse met her at the gate, ears pricked forward, large brown eyes full of curiosity.

"Ready for some adventure, girl?" She stroked the mare's muzzle. Chancy reached for the horse's bridle and slipped the bit into the mare's mouth, then pushed the headstall over her soft ears.

She unlatched the stall gate and led Bowie out. Within moments, her horse was saddled, and Chancy led her faithful mount into the turbulence of the night.

At least the thunder has moved away. She stared into the sky. The heavens were still dark and steady raindrops pounded her hat and shoulders, but the storm had calmed for a moment. With a deep breath to steady herself, she pulled herself into the saddle.

With a nudge of her heels, the mare trotted into the darkness. *Here I go...* Chancy hoped her plan would work. If not, she'd be on her way to Omaha by the end of the week.

The trail in the dark held a sinister atmosphere and with each passing minute became more difficult to traverse. There were any number of dangers that lurked about which could injure her or Bowie, or worse, with every step.

The hair rose on the back of her neck and her heart pounded in her ears, but determination kept her moving forward. Instead of riding through the pastures to where she knew Nick was staying, she decided to risk a shortcut through the mountainous part of the ranch.

The terrain was rocky, with craggy cliffs and large boulders to ride around. To her growing horror the thunder had returned with a vengeance. Bowie kept a steady forward pace with trained diligence. "Good girl." She stroked the mare's shoulder.

A heavy rain with a sharp edge fell, pelting down upon her and Bowie. She tucked her chin to her chest and slumped her shoulders forward in an attempt to protect herself against the deluge. The lightening struck the ground closer and closer to the trail and now it seemed the thunder was directly overhead.

The thunder let loose a loud boom, and the ground shook beneath them. Rocks from the cliffs she rode by hurdled down the hill, landing all around them. Chancy wondered if she'd be sick. *I've made a bad decision,* but now there was no turning back.

Chancy clenched her teeth to hold in a scream. *Help,* her mind called, but there would be no one near who would be able to hear her. The ground became muddy and slick; fast-moving streams now flowed underfoot. She couldn't remember if this trail flash flooded. She knew of this trail, but had never ridden this direction in the past. She racked her mind trying to recall. Waterfalls cascaded over rock bluffs to converge with the ever-growing stream which swirled about her horse's feet. *I need to get out of here.*

The storm still ravaged the night sky. Along with the thunder and lightning a gust of wind blew through the bluff's stealing the hat from her head and blowing it into the darkness. Her loose hair whisked about her and stuck to her face. She brushed away the wet strands and scanned the darkness for her hat. It was long gone. With a discouraged grunt she nudged Bowie ahead.

The horse's hooves slipped and slid on the mud and rocks. She was in a creek bed of some sort she realized as the water now reached Bowie's hocks and continued to grow deeper with each passing moment. In the dark, she was unsure how much farther she'd be in this stretch of trail. Danger whispered in her ear. A feeling of helplessness threatened to consume her.

Not one to give up without a fight, she continued to navigate Bowie along the trail in the shadowy darkness. She could no longer hear above the fierceness of the wind and the rain which continued to pound the earth in angry torrents.

Maybe I should just go home, panic clutched at her heart. It's not worth me or Bowie getting hurt. There must be a way to change her parents' minds about sending her away. But her father's face flashed in her mind. No, he'll never change. His decision was made, she could tell by the set of his shoulders and the gleam in his eyes. Her only hope would be Nick. If she could convince him to help her.

The reins tightened in Chancy's hands. Bowie slipped and fell to her knees. She attempted to steady her by shifting her weight toward the horse's haunches. The mare screamed in terror, the sound turned Chancy's blood to ice in her veins.

Her body was thrust forward in the saddle, her boot lost its grip in the stirrup and her body slipped to the side of the horse. The sudden movement sent both she and Bowie off the edge of the trail.

The ground gave way, and they slid down the embankment. The rocks, jagged and unmoving, dug into her side as she slid inches in front of her horse down the bank.

Chancy came to an abrupt halt against a rock. It was cold and wet against her side. She coughed and gasped for a breath. Bowie let out a squeal that curled her toes. The fallen horse thrashed about on her side, her hooves slicing into the air. In its attempt to stand, the horse's body shoved her against the boulder, leaving her immobilized.

Pain. It radiated throughout her body, hard and fast. Chancy gulped for air. Each breath was a struggle. She attempted to wiggle her toes, her right foot was numb, jolts of pain radiated up her leg.

With a deep breath she leaned forward and touched her foot. The movement stole her breath away, and she had a moment of dizziness. Stars blinked before her eyes.

Chancy lay back. She squeezed her eyes shut. *Don't panic. Think!* Bowie had managed to stand.

The horse took several steps away from her. "Bowie, don't leave me, girl." Chancy's heart raced—if her horse spooked, she'd be stranded. The horse moved forward, its steps hesitant. She could see Bowie favored her back leg.

At that moment, Chancy tasted the salty wetness of her tears, mixed with the rain. Another clap of thunder resounded across the land. Spooked, Bowie reared, hooves striking the air before she disappeared into the darkness. Alone, and on the verge of panic, Chancy became faint.

She rested her head against the coolness of the rock. *What now?* The rain fell in steady sheets, the lightning since diminished into the distance. Her body was numb. Tired, she was so tired. Giving into the need, she closed her eyes and dozed.

***

Nick sat at the small table, sipping lukewarm coffee he made earlier in the morning as he waited for the fire he just built, to warm the small room. Bones lay at his feet, steam rising from his fur. The line shack was built solid with plenty of mud between the logs of the outside of the building to insulate the small space. Soon, the chill of the room dissipated and warmth once again soothed his body.

The thunderous storm he'd rode through earlier as he checked the cattle had moved farther south, and now a steady rainfall beat against the roof. The sound was calming and his eyelids became heavy as the warmth of the fire and the coffee surged through his body. Bones stirred at his feet, and lay on his side, legs stretched out before him.

Nick's several weeks in these mountains had cleared his mind of the indecision he'd been consumed with in his heart. Chancy was a large part of this indecision. Over the months since he'd joined the ranch, he'd grown quite fond of the girl. *Girl* being the key word.

Though he felt a kindred spirit toward her, she was still young. Her father had higher hopes for her future than with a ranch hand and wanderer, such as he. Her father would most likely prefer a rich city boy from Omaha as her future beau, than a homeless drifter.

It was time to move on in search of his own future. Though young as she was, Chancy had taught him much in his time here. She was brave and adventurous, not one to let anything set her back.

Things he much admired in the girl. In the morning, he would return to the ranch. Let Jim Mallory know he would collect his pay and be on his way. Farther west, toward the great ocean folks talked about. Then, maybe head north a spell, and see what the land offered there. The possibilities were endless in his mind.

Nick pulled back the quilt on the cot in the single room. Bones jumped on the bed and wagged his tail. "Down boy, you're still wet." The dog jumped down and nudged his leg with his cold snout.

"I'll let you up here in a minute." He smiled down at his faithful friend. Bones was good company on these lonely nights. He blew out the lantern on the small table beside the bed and sat down. He pulled off his boots and socks, arranging them for easy access in the morning. Disrobed, he lay on his side, and pulled the quilt to his chin. Bones jumped back on the quilt and made himself at home near Nick's feet.

Nick rolled onto his back and stared into the darkness, his hands behind his head. Already, his heart ached. The thought of leaving Chancy made him miserable. They were so close to being ready for her to ride the colt, Snowbar, to the ranch. The mustang responded well to her. She was a natural with horses, that, he couldn't deny. *When I return, I'll have Chancy show her father her secret before I leave.* This calmed his heart. Sated, he fell into a deep sleep.

With morning came a stream of sunlight through the lone window of the line shack. Nick rose on his elbow and looked about. Bones waited by the door and gave a reminding bark. Nick hopped out of bed to let his friend outside to do his business.

Today, he would ride back to the ranch. First, he'd find Chancy, tell her today was the day to show her father the colt. Then, he'd tell them his news. He would be leaving. With any luck, Chancy's father would be so impressed with his daughter, he'd change his mind about her future and the ranch. He hoped, for Chancy's sake.

He straightened the room before he left for the next man who'd be sent here. With a final glance around, he stepped outside into the heat of the morning, Bones at his heels. It would be a warm day, already the suns rays beat against the ground, drying the dampness from the night before.

Nick walked to the corral and shelter where his horse rested. The gelding saw him and gave a nicker of recognition when he neared. "Hey, boy. Ready to go home?" The horse shook his head, mane flowing with the movement.

Horse saddled, Nick filled his canteen from the flowing stream behind the shack. He stroked his friend's shoulder before he pulled himself into the saddle. A hint of sadness clouded his heart as he rode away. He would miss this place and the solitude he'd found when here.

His horse kept a steady pace on the trail home. Though warm outside, the rains of the night before made the trail slick in areas, and the meadows were boggy, sucking the horse's hooves into the earth, making it difficult to cross.

Nick whistled a tune to pass the time. He enjoyed the quiet, but on occasion it was nice to have a little noise, even if he was the one who made it. He glanced around at the surroundings. Bones barked and was on the trail of a rabbit which happened to hop in front of their path. "Bones," he called but, it was useless. The dog would return when he tired of the chase.

The closer to the ranch they came, the less mountainous the terrain became. His horse's ears pricked forward, his body tensed beneath him. Nick raised his hand to shield his eyes from the sun while he scanned the area. Bones was most likely going to run out of the tall grass, tongue lolling against his lip. But in caution he reached for the rifle in the scabbard at his horse's side.

"Bones?" he called. The dog did not return. He continued to ride forward, his horse snorted and swished his tail, ears pinned against his head. Nick's keen eye surveyed the area but nothing was out of place. Then a movement in the distance caught his eye. A lone horse, saddled and limping through the meadow. *Bowie?* "What the..."

CHAPTER FIFTEEN

Nick spurred his mount into a swift gallop. The horse in the distance looked very much like Bowie to his growing concern. *What would Chancy be doing out here this time of day?* As he approached the horse, he realized the saddle was askew, and the mare limped a few pathetic steps at a time. She stopped when she caught the scent of Nick's horse.

Bowie raised her head and let out a loud whinny in their direction. Nick raced to the horse and jumped off the side of his own mount. He sprinted the last few steps and grabbed for Bowie's broken reins which dragged on the ground.

"Where's Chancy, girl?" Nick scanned the area stroking the injured horse's neck.

"Chancy...Chancy," he called. There was no response. He ran his hand along Bowie's shoulder then on toward her hindquarter. "Easy, girl." The saddle was loosened enough it now hung under her belly. The horse flinched when he reached for the cinch. In quiet tones, he calmed her while he unfastened the saddle, letting it fall to the ground. Bowie nudged his shoulder with her nose. "I know, girl, that wasn't very comfortable."

He stroked her forehead then gave her another pat on the shoulder. "Good girl, now where's your mistress?" He scanned the area one last time. There was no sign of Chancy anywhere. He led Bowie to where he'd left his own horse. With each step Bowie took, he noticed how extensive her limp was.

He stopped and went to examine her leg further. The mare's back hindquarter and lower leg were swollen twice the normal size he noticed. He ran his hands down the sides of her leg, heat radiated to his hands. She'd need care and rest to heal from this.

With a sigh, he led the horse forward once more. They'd

have to walk slow and easy. Dread clutched at his heart. *Where's Chancy, is she laying somewhere hurt?* She'd never leave her horse unattended. *Something bad has happened.* Discouraged, he ran his hands through his hair.

Bones appeared a few moments later panting from his escapade through the tall grasses. "Here, boy," he called the dog to his side. He knelt on his knee and scratched the dog behind the ear. *I have to find her.* Mind made up, Nick stood and removed Bowie's bridle and tied his own horse to a tree limb.

He'd search the area on foot, and hopefully with Bones help he'd find his friend.

"Chancy—Chancy, can you hear me?" Nick called out, while he searched the surrounding areas of the meadow. "Bones, find her, buddy," he commanded the dog. The dog rushed away snout to the dirt with a low whimper. Hours later, there was still no sign of Chancy. Nick wiped a bead of sweat from his brow. He needed to check the horses where he'd left them in the meadow. He'd walked several miles around the location where he'd found Bowie and found nothing. Failure had never tasted so bitter.

Discouraged and thirsty, Nick reached for his canteen hanging from the saddle horn on his horse. He drank long and heartily then poured some of the cool drink into his hand for Bones to drink. *I have to go back to the ranch for help.* It was the only thing he could think to do. The more men who joined the search the quicker they'd find Chancy.

Nick left Bowie in the meadow, he'd return for her later. Recruiting help was the most important thing he could do right now. He mounted his horse and with Bones at his feet, he kicked the horse into a run.

Sliding to a stop in front of the main ranch house, Nick jumped off the side of his horse. He took the porch steps two at a time until he was face to face with the closed door. With several hard knocks he waited. Alma Mallory opened the door, her features flushed, a surprised look on her face.

"Nick?" concern laced her voice.

"Mrs. Mallory—is Mr. Mallory inside? Please, it's urgent."

The woman opened the door wider, "Yes, he's in his office. Please come inside."

Nick removed his hat and placed it before him as he stepped inside the house. He quickly strode down the hall and into Jim's office. "Mr. Mallory, something's happened to Chancy." The man's head shot up from the books he was reviewing.

Breathless, Nick continued. "I found Bowie in the meadows, her saddle askew and she was limping. I searched the area for several hours and never found any sign of Chancy. Something bad's happened to her, I'm afraid, sir, so I came back to get help."

Jim stood from his desk, the papers he'd been reading floated to the floor around him. "Go out and gather some men and horses. We'll ride back out and start another search."

"Yes, sir." Nick trotted back out of the office and out the front door. He gathered his horse's reins, mounted, then galloped down the path to the barn. An hour later with every ranch hand saddled and ready to ride, the group rode out in search of Chancy. They split into two groups, one headed for the mountains, the other toward the meadows where Nick had found Bowie earlier in the day.

Nick rode with Slim and several other hands he bunked with. They rode for the meadows at a gallop. Once they reached the location where he'd found Bowie, they split up to cover more ground.

Nick turned his horse to the direction of where he and Chancy had hidden the colt in the mustang enclosure. He wondered if Chancy had tried to handle the colt by herself in his absence.

When he reached the corral where they'd kept the mustang, he found it empty. *The storm must have scared the colt enough to rush the fence,* Nick thought, bile churning in his gut. A section of poles was splintered where the horse had pushed through.

"Unbelievable," he muttered, pulling a tuft of white hair

from the wood. He stepped inside the enclosure to search the area. Several more poles were covered in hair and blood. He hoped the colt wasn't injured too severely. He prayed they'd find Chancy soon and that she'd be unharmed.

***

Chancy awoke stiff and chilled to the bone. The heat of the day hadn't warmed her much where she'd landed, hidden in the shadows of several large boulders. Her ribs hurt from colliding with the rock earlier, and her foot, she realized was swollen inside her boot. It hurt to move. "Help—help," she croaked, but there was no reply.

Her surroundings were sparse. Boulders and rocks of varying sizes lay strung about between tufts of sagebrush. She was in a ravine of some sort. The earth was still damp from the previous night's storm. Her thoughts went to Bowie. Was she okay? Had she returned to the ranch? Surely her father was out searching for her right now, wasn't he?

With a grunt and good dose of stubborn will, she pulled herself to her feet. A white-hot blaze of pain shot through her system, and for a moment stars circled before her eyes. *I can do this.* She took a step forward, the weight of her body shifting to her injured leg.

The world darkened before her, and she fell to her knees. "Help me," she yelled. Over and over, she screamed the words until her throat hurt and her voice was hoarse. *Please, let them find me.* Tears of frustration ran down her face, adding to the dampness on the ground.

Her leg now throbbed clear to the knee. "I need to get this boot off." She grunted. Her foot throbbed with each heartbeat and she wondered if it would explode inside the boot. Leaning forward, she untied the bootlaces. The swelling was so advanced she couldn't shove the boot off. Red hot currents of pain blazed before her eyes, sweat had gathered at her brow with each movement.

You can do this Chancy—you have to. Steadying herself, she found a crevice between a rock and a boulder. Scooting forward on her backside, she placed her foot into the divot. Closing her eyes and holding her breath, she pulled with all her might, until her foot came out of the entrapment.

Breathless and panting, Chancy rested her weight on her elbows. Already her foot throbbed less without the constriction of the boot. When she caught her wind again, she crawled to the shelter of the boulders once more; protection from the heat. She dozed off and on, every so often calling out, but still there was no return answer.

Chancy watched a hawk in the distance. The graceful bird floated in the air with wild beauty. *If I could only fly home. Stop this childishness, it's time to start thinking about survival.* She had no food and no water, an injured leg and was hidden in a steep ravine away from the eyes of those who she suspected were searching for her.

She needed to take action, move away from the confines of this rocky alcove. She needed a stick of some kind to use as a crutch. Searching the ground, to her dismay, she found nothing. The only other option was to crawl on her hands and knees. Unable to come up with a better solution, she went down on all fours and started to move forward.

After several minutes, her hands were cut and bruised, her knees ached and bled from gashes caused by the sharp rocks. She bit her lip to hold back more tears threatening to pour forth. *I have to get out of here.* Pushing the pain to the back of her mind, she crawled on.

The ravine went on and on, with sharp winds and turns, Chancy realized after a few more minutes. She needed to pull herself back to higher ground, the trail above that Bowie and she had traversed before they'd slid over the side. She grabbed for a scraggly sagebrush and pulled herself up, using rocks like stepping stones.

When she'd reached the top, once again she was breathless and drenched in sweat, but she'd managed to accomplish this task. She lay a few minutes longer until her heart rate steadied and she could breathe normal once more. The sun had disappeared over the mountain during her laborious climb. Darkness would soon shroud the land. "Help—help," she tried again.

The sight of a large Ponderosa pine just off the trail caught her eye. She could use the bed of pine needles covering the ground around the base like a blanket. She crawled forward until she reached the tree and could rest her back against the trunk. She grabbed handfuls of the scratchy pine needles and covered herself the best she could. Even if the days were warm, the nights could be brutal from the chill.

An owl hooted in the distance. The world was now dark; the shadows of the night ominous. It appeared she'd be spending another night in the wild. In the past, this wouldn't have bothered her. But injured, hungry, and tired, it felt like the world had come to an end.

Hours later, how many she was unsure, a noise had awakened her from her slumber. What was that? Her heart raced as she strained her eyes in search of what may be ahead. "Hello? Hello?" No one returned her call. Instead, she quieted and continued to listen, see if the noise occurred again.

Silence was the answer, but she shivered in both fear and cold. Her body was numb from the elements, but the pine needles helped. Morning couldn't be too far off. An early morning light cast its shadow over the mountains in the distance. Her father would be searching for her once again at first light. Of this she was sure.

CHAPTER SIXTEEN

"Chancy—Chanceee,"

Had she heard right? Or was the sound just another ghost voice in the wind? Chancy lifted her chin and listened. When the call no longer sounded again, she fought the despair that threatened to take over her mind. She was cold and half-starved. The pain in her leg no longer bothered her compared to the knife wrenching ache in her gut from hunger, or the prickly spines in her throat from thirst.

Her head slumped forward, chin on her chest when the call came again. This time the sound was loud and clear. "Chanceee." Her father's voice.

"I'm here—I'm here!" She struggled to dislodge the words from her throat. With all the effort she could muster, she pulled herself onto her feet. Stars circled before her eyes, but she refused to give into the darkness.

"Pa, Pa, I'm here," she tried again. Seconds later, her father appeared out of the mists, several men on horseback behind him. He galloped to her side and dismounted before his horse could slide to a halt.

"Oh, Chancy, I've been so worried. We thought you...Well we thought you might not have made it sweetheart." With tears in his eyes, he pulled her into his warm embrace. Never had her father's arms felt so warm and comforting as they did right now.

"I didn't think anyone was going to find me. Bowie and I were on this trail when she slipped. We went over the ravine...Is she okay?" She pulled back to look into her father's face. Fear of what may have become of her horse tormented her.

"Nick found Bowie. I think she was all right. She was in a meadow, injured. Nick searched for hours for you, but when he came up empty-handed, he had to leave her behind and ride for help. I'm sure Nick will find her and take good care of her for you. He has a way with horses."

"I know, Pa..." But her heart broke anyway with the knowledge her decision had cost her horse an injury.

"We had every man out searching for you." Her father eyes glittered with unshed tears, and he pulled her tight into his arms once again.

"Someone bring me a blanket, she's half frozen." Her father called out to the men.

One of the hands pulled a blanket from behind the cantle of his saddle and tossed it to her father. The warmth of the wool steadied her nerves and her thoughts became clear once again.

"Oh, Pa. I was so scared. I didn't think anyone would be able to find me. Last night was the longest night of my life." She shivered at the memory.

"Let's get you home, so your ma can fuss over you. You do look a sight girl, your face is a mudpie, and the rest of you is scratched and covered in dried blood. Are there any other injuries we may have missed?"

"I think I may have twisted or broken my ankle. I'm not sure which. And, when Bowie and I slid down the hill, I was crushed against a boulder. Some of my ribs are mighty sore." She lifted her foot so he could see. She hadn't been brave enough to glance at it yet this morning herself. She couldn't bear the thought her ankle might be broken.

When she did look, her foot was grotesquely swollen, bright shades of black, blue and purple hues. Not a pretty sight.

"Does it hurt as bad as it looks?"

Chancy grimaced at her father's question. "It hurts like the dickens. I tried to put weight on it yesterday and thought I'd pass out. I can't seem to put any weight on it right now."

Her father pulled her into his arms and carried her to his horse. "Can you ride all right by yourself?"

Chancy positioned herself in the saddle, leaving her injured leg swinging at the horse's side. "I think so. My foot's too swollen to put into the stirrup though."

"I'll ride behind you then. We don't need the horse spooking and you losing your balance and falling off breaking something else."

"Do you think I broke my leg, Pa?" If she had, she'd be laid up in bed for weeks. Not her idea of a good time, especially with summer's end approaching fast. This year's summer with Nick and the colt had passed too quickly as it was.

"That'll be the doctor's decision when we get you home." Her father pulled himself into the saddle behind her. He positioned the blanket around her shoulders until she was tucked in like a baby and pressed firmly against his chest.

On the ride home, Chancy flitted in and out of sleep. Her dreams were vivid and so lifelike she wondered if she'd called out in her sleep. In her dream, the colt Snowbar, ran about the mustang enclosure in a panic. His hooves struck the air with each clash of thunder across the blackened sky. He ran and bucked his defiance at the storm.

When a great bolt of lightning struck a tree not far from where he'd slid to a stop, fear urged him forward. He ran, and ran, not stopping for the poles that held together the enclosure. He jumped, but was unable to clear the fence. His chest took out the top rail. The wood snapped and splintered in two. The horse screamed in pain and anguish, but did not stop. Instead, he disappeared into the darkness of the night.

***

Chancy awakened to the comfort of quilts, her mother's goose down quilts at that, wrapped around her body tight and snug. Perspiration dotted her forehead. A dream had left her heart racing, a cry of anguish on her lips. *Snowbar, did he escape that horrible night? Was he okay?* She needed to speak with Nick.

"You're awake." Alma stepped into the room and walked to her bedside. "Oh, Chancy. We've all been so worried about you." Her mother's face softened a tinge before fear took over, then anger. "First you run off in the middle of the night during the worst storm we've seen in ages, and then you twist your ankle and bruise your ribs enough to need to keep you bedridden for a week. What should we do with you child?"

A small smile formed on Chancy's lips. "So, my leg's not broken? Just a twisted ankle?" What a relief. A twisted ankle just needed a little rest. And bruised ribs, well she'd experienced those before from a fall from an oak tree when she was younger and survived. She'd be up and mobile in no time.

"Just a twisted ankle? Do you know how lucky you are Chancy? Things could have been so much worse."

"That's not what I meant, Ma. I know a twisted ankle is not a good thing. I just thought I'd be bed ridden for the rest of summer."

Her mother stared long and hard at her, then a strange expression overtook her features. One Chancy had never experienced before.

"You better have some lunch. You'll need the food to regain your strength."

Chancy couldn't argue that. "Thanks, Ma."

Alma set a tray next to her bed. The plate boasted a sandwich with a side of cookies. Her mother's special chocolate cookies she only baked on certain occasions.

"Did I miss something?" Chancy asked with surprise.

"What do you mean?" Her mother raised her eyebrows.

"The cookies—we normally only get these on special occasions: birthdays, Thanksgiving and such."

"Well, I thought you being found alive, was a call for a *special* occasion."

"Oh," Chancy replied.

"I'll be back in a while to check on you, Chancy. I'm sure your father will be up soon to speak with you." With those final words her mother disappeared outside her door.

"Ma, is Nick around?" she called out before her mother was out of earshot.

Her mother paused outside the doorway. "I'll ask your father, I'm not sure. I know he's the one who found Bowie and brought her home. She also has an injured leg, but you should be able to ride her again in the future."

"Gosh...," hearing Bowie was injured was painful.

Alone, once more in her room, Chancy stared out her bedroom window. The day was bright, and the sunlight lightened her room. She turned on her side and sighed. Her adventure of the day before had left her exhausted and confused.

"Hey, Chancy, can I come in?"

The voice was Anna's. Chancy sighed. She didn't want to have any more awkwardness between them. Since Nick had arrived, their relationship had changed. They'd become distant.

"Sure," Chancy finally replied.

"I'm sorry about Bowie and your accident," Anna said and moved closer to her bed.

"Thanks, I'm feeling better, and I've been told Bowie will be fine."

Silence ensued. Chancy looked at her friend. Anna wore her normal carefree smile. This made her relax somewhat. She feared Anna would be put out with her over Nick.

"Well, I should go. I just wanted to check on you and see for myself you were okay."

"Thanks," Chancy said, then became silent once more.

"Oh, and I thought I would tell you while I'm here. I've moved on from Nick. When I was at the church social, the one Nick escorted me to, I met a new boy who has recently moved to these parts. His name is Warren Mills. Chancy, he is so wonderful. He's come to visit twice this week. I can't wait for you to meet him."

"That sounds great, Anna. I'm happy for you." Chancy's heart lightened with this news.

"Talk with you later then." Anna stepped to the door.

"Thanks for stopping in," Chancy called out as Anna disappeared outside of her room. Maybe things were about to change for the better. She could always hope.

CHAPTER SEVENTEEN

Nick stepped out of the barn and into the heat of the day. He'd finished grooming Bowie and tending her leg injury. She would heal with time, which relieved him. If the horse had damaged her leg any further she'd have needed to be put down. Nick stared ahead; Jim Mallory strode his way, a look of grim determination on his face. It was time.

"Mr. Mallory, if I could speak with you?" The man paused and looked at him, his face an unreadable mask.

"Sure, son, meet me in my office at the house in half an hour. I need to talk with Deacon about a few matters first."

"Thank you, sir." Nick watched his boss continue by. *Should I speak with Chancy before or after I tell Jim?* His heart was undecided. Over the last few months he'd come to care for the wild and adventurous girl. In fact, he knew she'd stolen his heart. It would hurt to leave her, and he knew she'd be angry when he told her his plan.

There's no other choice. I must move on. Bones whined near his feet. The lovable pup sensed his unease, his dark brown eyes gazed up at him. Nick leaned down and gave his faithful companion a scratch on top of his head. Mind set, he lumbered toward the bunkhouse to finish packing the last of his meager belongings.

The dreaded walk to the ranch house set Nick on edge. He didn't like goodbyes. In fact, he'd left his parents with only a short note of goodbye when he'd left them all those months ago now. He'd just about done the same to Chancy, but something held him back from doing so; a small inkling that in the future, he might return.

The idea had surfaced the night before, when he'd lain awake on his bunk and relived his past months on the ranch;

his time with Chancy. He would travel further north maybe and settle down with his own piece of land. Give a go at ranching. When he settled in and built a name for himself, he'd return. Return for Chancy—if she'd have him.

***

Jim had yet to return to his office when Nick entered. He stepped inside anyhow and gazed at
the many paintings which graced the walls. Paintings of great horseflesh. Nick had been told Alma was an artist and had painted most of the pictures, but several of the newer paintings had been painted by Chancy.

He could see the wildness in her artwork. One, a picture of a herd of mustangs running across a snowy meadow. She managed to capture the essence of the wild horses' grace and strength on the paper. Stunning.

"Chancy has a lot of talent, does she not?"

Nick turned as Jim stepped inside his office. The man walked behind his desk and sat down before the large desk, his hands folded in front of him.

"Yes, sir, she does." Nick was still in awe of the breathtaking scene. But he turned from the paintings. It was time to speak his mind.

"I wanted to let you know, I'll be leaving today. I'm going to make my way farther north and see if I can't start my own homestead. I need to make my own way in this world, and I believe I'm ready."

Jim didn't appear surprised by this information. He cleared his throat and looked Nick in the eye.

"You're an excellent horseman, Nick. I think with time and experience you'll be quite a contender in the horse world with your skills. It's a shame you must leave, but I agree, this will be for the best."

Nick hadn't been sure what the man's words would be with his news of leaving, but he hadn't expected things to go so smoothly.

Before he lost his nerve, he dove in deeper. "I would like

to ask your permission, sir, and Chancy's of course; in the future, the next couple of years I'm thinking, to give myself time to become settled." He cleared his throat again. "I'd like to call on Chancy." Nick's heart rate slowed, and he held his breath while he awaited the man's answer.

Jim became very still behind his desk. His hand went to his mustache and twirled the hair

between his thumb and index finger. Nick's heart thundered in his ears while he waited.

"I'll keep that in mind."

Nick let out a breath of relief.

"You're a good boy, Nick. I like you a lot, but as you know, Chancy is a bit of a rogue. I sometimes wonder how much I can really control her. She's a strong mind and a wild heart. I'm sure you'll have a time of it taming that girl." Jim shook his head, a smile on his lips.

"If Chancy agrees after you speak to her of this, in a couple of years, when she turns eighteen, you have my blessing to come calling on her if she so desires.

Nick extended his hand. "Thank you, sir. This means a lot to me."

Jim grasped his hand and gave it a powerful shake. "Its been good knowing you, son. I wish you the best of luck in the future."

With a parting tip of his hat, Nick stepped outside of the office and rested his back against the closed door. He hadn't realized sweat trickled down his back. Now for the hardest part. Saying goodbye to Chancy.

He reached the door to her room and paused mid-step. A coward he had never been, but the urge to run and never look back coursed through him faster than a rabbit escaping its hunter. With a deep breath, he took the plunge and knocked on her closed door.

"Come in," a soft voice called out. Nick savored the coolness of the doorknob under his palm and opened the door. Chancy's face brightened when she realized who her visitor was.

"Nick, I've been waiting for you. Where have you been? I have so many questions." Her animated features lightened his heart. Chancy was easy to be with and lightened the darkness he carried around his heart.

"I meant to come sooner, but had other business to tend first."

"You mean speaking with my father? He just left here a while ago, said you'd asked to speak with him. Is everything all right?"

Nick groaned inwardly with her question. *No, everything is not all right.* I've gone and let myself fall for this girl. Her cheeks were flushed, her brown eyes sparkled with life. He'd need all his strength to walk away.

"I came here to..." the words wouldn't budge from his lips, "I came here to tell you that...I'm leaving."

The smile quickly disappeared from her lips, faster than a raging storm overtakes a sunny day. Her eyes clouded and glimmered with unshed tears.

"You can't leave, Nick! What about Snowbar and his training?" She looked at him expectantly.

He hadn't yet told her about Snowbar's escape with the storm. The news was sure to send her over the edge.

"I checked the mustang enclosure when we searched for you. Snowbar is gone. He must have bolted during the storm. I found some blood and tufts of hair on the shattered poles he jumped over."

Her face crumpled before him. "I'm so sorry, Chancy."

She sniffed, but the tears he'd expected didn't fall. Instead a stony mask covered her features.

Anger and hurt still shone through in equal quantities. She tilted her head so he could no longer see her face. Silence filled the room, uncomfortable and toxic.

"Well, I should be going then." He took a hesitant step backward toward the door.

"Just like that? You're going to leave me?" Her angry words clawed at his heart.

"Please understand. It's something I need to do." She wasn't going to take this news well, he could sense by the tone of her voice.

"I'm sorry, Nick. I thought you were my friend." Her breath caught, "maybe even something more." She lowered her eyes, the fight draining away.

"Chancy, please listen to me."

"No, Nick. Please go, have a good life." She'd cut him off, tried to severe the cord of friendship.

He couldn't believe how cold her words were. *I deserve this,* he reminded himself. She couldn't really mean what she'd said, could she? But, she had given him no room for argument. He'd leave her now, but he'd be back, ready to fight for her heart.

***

Chancy listened to the echo of Nick's boots against the hardwood floors as he walked down the hallway. When she was sure he was gone, the tears came. Great torrents of them. *How could he leave me?* Anger, frustration, and deceit swirled around in her mind.

"Dang him..." She reached for the book on her bedside table and threw it at the wall across the room. She took her blankets and pillows and threw them to the floor. Still, fury and the painful throb of the truth surged through her.

I will not let this be a setback. The simple promise to herself sounded so shallow. If she could only walk right now, she'd chase him down, confront him on his decision. Couldn't he see that he belonged here?

Her first impressions of him had been wrong. And to have been jealous of him...Nick was the best thing that could have happened. Her father thought he was amazing with horses, he was a hard worker, someone who would keep the ranch running.

Then a sudden thought hit her like a punch in the gut. The air was sucked from her lungs. He couldn't stay, this land was not his, would never be his. It was hers. Legends of old said ranch hands would never marry into a ranch owner's family. At least not ranch hands with any self-worth. Nick was lost to her. Forever. Once again, tears streamed down her cheeks.

Several minutes later, the onslaught of tears over, Chancy sat up in bed. She gazed out the window toward the barn. Her heart stopped, her breath caught in her throat. Nick led his horse out of the barn, Bones playfully nipping at his heels.

He checked his cinch, his bridle, then reached down and rubbed the dog affectionately on the head. Was he stalling for time? *Why doesn't he just get on and ride away?* Chancy's gaze was glued to the window.

Nick raised his chin and stared toward the house. Toward her bedroom. *Can he see me? See how he's breaking my heart?* His face was shadowed by his hat, but his lips were a thin, grim line. He gathered the reins into his hand and put his boot into the stirrup pulling himself into the saddle.

There he goes. Chancy wondered if her heart could break into any more pieces. Dust plumes rose up from the ground as he trotted out of sight of her window, his dog faithful at his side. Then he was gone...

***

The next several days passed without notice, Chancy was in a self-induced daze of self pity. A type of depression she'd never experienced before. Even her parents stared at her with their faces full of worry when they thought she wasn't looking. She couldn't help her listless, quiet behavior; didn't know how to fix these emotions.

She realized with a start, she'd been staring out the window into the distance for hours. *What do I expect, Nick to return—say he was wrong?* She knew that would never be. Nick was too proud and resilient to do such a thing.

"Chancy, your mother and I have discussed you leaving for Omaha. We think with all the recent incidents it would be better if you remained at the ranch. This is your home. Your future, I realize, is here." Her father paused, a look of hope on his face. Expectation, she was sure, that she'd snap out of this deep, cavernous despair she'd fallen into.

She moved her gaze from the window to his intense stare.

He twirled his mustache between his fingers. This brought a small smile to her lips. The familiarity of her father and his predictable habits.

"Thank you, Pa. You don't know how much those words means to me." She turned her gaze back to the window.

"Doc said yesterday, after his visit, he thought you're healed enough to start moving about. The men have fashioned a crutch to help you, so you can walk to the barn and visit Bowie. I know she misses you. Every time one of the hands or even myself steps into the barn, she's looking for you."

Chancy cringed at hearing this, in her misery she hadn't bothered to ask about her beloved horse. "Pa, would you help me out to the barn this afternoon?"

"Sure, sweetheart. I'll have your mother bring you some lunch while I go tend to a few chores, then I'll be back and walk you to the barn." Her pa leaned in and kissed her forehead. "It's good to have you back, sweetheart."

CHAPTER EIGHTEEN

Nick scanned the horizon. He'd been on the trail of the band of mustangs for three days now. At first, he'd brushed away the idea of trying to recapture Snowbar. But, as he watched the gallant steed race across the wind- swept prairie, wind in his mane, horseflesh, grace and power, he knew he had to catch the horse. Return him to Chancy. It was the least he could do.

Now, he crouched against the cool exterior of a boulder, watching and waiting for his chance. His own horse, he'd left in a cluster of trees several lengths back. He would need to swoop in on the herd, try to separate Snowbar from his band and lasso him. Sounded easy enough, but he understood the dangers of this plight all too well.

After several minutes of watching, it was time. Nick returned to his horse and mounted. He pulled on his leather gloves and removed the lariat from the side of his saddle. He swung a loop over his head to ready himself before he spurred his horse into a gallop and started after the herd.

Luck may be on my side today. His pulse thundered. The colt was already separated from the band. Nick, low over his horse's neck, reined the mount toward him, keeping himself on the inside, a barrier between Snowbar and the mustangs. The colt stood rooted, ears forward, tail raised in the wind.

His dark spots glistened against the white of his coat.

"Easy, boy," Nick whispered, his voice lost in the wind. Closer, closer, just a little closer. Every muscle in Nick's body was taught, poised and ready. He swung the rope. His aim was true, he quickly dallied the lariat around his saddle horn. His cow pony, trained in the art of subduing cattle, skidded to a halt, keeping the rope taught.

Snowbar fought a gallant fight. He reared, bucked,

snorted, and darted. Anything to get away, but Nick's horse held true, not letting the rope grow slack. To Nick's great relief, Snowbar soon tired.

He stood facing Nick, his hide covered in a sheen of sweat and foam. He snorted and heaved for each breath. The smell of horseflesh was thick in the air.

Nick reached down and rubbed his horse's shoulder. His own mount was in a lather, breathing hard as was Nick himself. He removed his hat and wiped the perspiration from his brow with the back of his hand. He'd done it.

With the skirmish, the other mustangs disappeared. All that remained was a distant dust cloud on the far horizon. His horse remained steady, and the colt calmed. Snowbar had been regrouped with his band for several weeks now. Will he resist my touch? Nick wondered if it'd be like starting over.

Nonplussed, he spoke in low tones to the youngster. Step-by-step, he worked his way closer and closer to the horse, hand outstretched.

The colt's ears pricked forward, eyes steady on him as he breathed heavily. Ever so slowly, Nick reached out and touched his side. The horse's skin rippled beneath his touch. "Easy, boy." His words were barely a whisper.

He slid his hand down the colt's neck, across his shoulders, to his haunches. He repeated the process several more times until the colt accepted his touch without flinching. "Good boy."

Exhilaration shot though his system with this victory. "You're going home to Chancy, my friend."

The thought of Chancy's smile when she laid eyes on her beloved mustang brightened Nick's spirits. Since he left the ranch, he'd traveled in a cloak of misery. He had recounted their last conversation over and over in his mind until he was sick from it. Returning Snowbar would be his chance for redemption in Chancy's eyes.

Hope restored, he fashioned a halter out of a length of rope he stored in his bedroll and slid it over the horse's ears, all the while speaking in smooth tones to the colt. Still somewhat skittish, Snowbar responded to his patience and slow movements and accepted his fate.

Three days later, after long days of working the colt from the ground to restore his trust, the colt once again accepted Nick's touch. On the fourth day, Nick took his saddle and set it on the colt's back.

He tightened the cinch and placed a bit into his mouth, sliding the headstall over his ears. Chancy had ridden the colt several times, but in the controlled area inside the mustang pen. Here, they were in the open, no rails to confine him.

The world seemed to quiet all around them when Nick placed his boot into the stirrup. "That's a boy," he cooed. Grabbing the saddle horn he pulled himself up and swung his leg over the colt's rump.

With minimal movement, he lowered himself into the saddle. When his bottom was firm in the seat, he let out his breath. He hadn't realized he'd been holding it. "Good boy," he patted the horse's shoulder.

Snowbar snorted and pawed the earth. With a gentle squeeze of his legs, the horse stepped forward. Light on the rein, Nick reined him in circles, each circle a bit larger, then he reversed the pattern.

"That's a good day's work." He halted Snowbar and dismounted. He couldn't wait to witness the excitement on Chancy's face when he returned the colt to her. The thought of her sent his mind into a jumble. When he was face to face with her again, he wanted to have control of his emotions. Leaving her a second time wouldn't be easy.

***

"Chancy, I'll walk with you to the barn." Her father stood against the door frame, a smile on his lips. Chancy stood. As of late the barn had done little to raise her bruised spirits. Since Nick's departure, she couldn't shake the gloomy fog she lived in.

"Doc said you should be able to start riding soon. The sprain's much improved. He was surprised you're still using the crutch."

Chancy's face flushed over this. She knew at some point she'd have to get back into the ranch's normal routine. She had a job to do, same as everyone else. And as of late, she'd neglected poor Bowie.

Another mark on her conscience.

"You're right, Pa. I was testing myself earlier, and I did fine without the crutch. Just a little limp."

"That's my girl." Her father grinned.

She hated the knowing look on his face. In fact it was a silly white lie to say her ankle still hurt at all. The last few days were pain free. She'd just needed a few more days to herself. To wallow in her self-pity.

Alma walked into the room, her face pale, a worried frown between her eyes. "We have a visitor, Jim."

"What's wrong, Alma? Who's here?" her father asked. He reached for Alma's hand in an attempt to comfort her.

"You better follow me." Alma turned and left the room, Jim behind her.

Chancy stood from the bed and followed her parents into the living room.

"Jim, this is Jedediah Stone. Nick's older brother."

Next to the window in her family's living room, a man stood, hands grasping his tan hat in front of him. Chancy froze in place. The stranger before her was a taller, brawnier version of Nick. Same facial features, long straight nose, crisp blue eyes. Soft baritone voice. An exact replica.

The man stepped forward and extended his hand. "Nice to meet you, Mr. Mallory. Sorry to intrude without notice. I was hoping my brother Nick might still be employed at your ranch."

Jim accepted the handshake, a worried expression shadowed his face.

"Maybe you should come into my office, Jedediah"

"Please, call me, Jed." He fell into step behind her father, and followed him down the hallway to his office at the back of the house.

Chancy paced in the living room. Alma sat on the couch and resumed her knitting.

"Chancy sit down, we'll know what his story is all in good time."

She couldn't sit down, couldn't concentrate, couldn't do anything. "Something bad's happened, I can sense it," she said aloud. Her stomach knotted with anxiety. How she'd love to be a fly on the wall in her father's office right now. Jed's appearance was a shock to her system.

"You're wearing a hole in my good rug, sit down, Chancy." Alma gave her a withered look.

"Yes, Ma." She sat on the couch and reached for something to read. Page by page, she browsed though the book from the side table, unable to concentrate on the words printed on the paper. Her mind wandered to all the reasons why Nick's brother would be searching for him. Nick had never discussed his family much. She knew he'd left them without telling them where he was going.

Her stomach clenched. Something had happened to one of his family members. Sorrow washed through her for Nick, and she didn't even know for sure this was what had occurred. The grim determined look on his brother's face, explained it all.

Moments later, Jim and Jed Stone walked into the living room both with equally bleak expressions on their faces.

"Let me tell them, sir, if you don't mind?" Jed looked at her father, who gave him a nod to go ahead.

Chancy took a deep breath to brace herself for what would be said.

"I came here in search of Nick for a reason. Our mother, well, she recently passed on..."

The rest of his words were cut short as Alma grasped her chest, her face deathly pale.

"I'm so sorry, you poor boys—please continue."

Jim walked over and pulled his wife into his arms. Jed cleared his throat and continued.

"It was my father's wish that I ride west to try and locate

Nick. He felt my brother should return to Boston and pay his respects to my mother's grave and visit his younger sister."

"Oh, I agree with your father. And I think, Nick, will want to do this. He's such a dear boy,"

Alma stated.

Chancy stood speechless. Nick's mother was dead. His brother was here to take him back east once more. Her mind tried to wrap around the concept.

"Jed, you're welcome to our spare guest room while you're here," Alma said. "I'll go get fresh linens and make up the bed."

"I appreciate your family's kindness," Jed stated. He appeared tired and was covered in a thick coat of dust from his travels.

"Chancy, get him fresh water in the basin, so he can freshen up, while I prepare the room." She stopped and looked at Jed. "Jim will take your horse to the barn and make sure it's fed and watered."

"Thanks again for all your hospitality."

Chancy left the room to do her mother's bidding. She wanted to question Jed, but he was tired from the trail. Her questions would have to wait.

"Chancy, you want to walk to the barn with me and help with Jed's horse?" her father asked.

"Sure, let me finish putting out this water." She hurried about her tasks, so she could go outside with her pa. He must have had something to discuss with her to ask her to do this.

Chancy and her father walked in silence toward the barn. Her father led Jed's trail weary horse.

Chancy stared into the sky. It was a deep blue, and the sun warmed the ground. A soft breeze blew the earthy smells of baked pine needles and berries past them. Soon, the wild berries would be ripe for the picking. One of her favorite house chores was to go with her mother and spend the afternoon picking wild berries. Then a nice picnic lunch beside the river, below the ever watchful graves of her brothers.

"Since you're doing so well today, why don't you take Bowie out for a ride. I bet it'll cheer you up," her father said, his lips pulled into a smirk.

Chancy looked up at her father. Worry lines crinkled around his eyes.

"Sounds good, Pa. I think I'll do it."

He gave her shoulder a soft squeeze before disappearing in front of her into the barn. Chancy paused and glanced in the distance. *Why do I look for him, he's not coming back.* She kicked a stray rock with the tip of her boot, then followed her father inside.

The sound of Bowie's soft nicker when she reached her stall warmed her heart. Bowie's love was unconditional. She scratched the mare behind her ears, then reached for her halter on a hook near the stall door and slipped it over her head.

Minutes later, to her great joy, she was once again running across the pasture, her hair unbound and flying behind her as she made her way to the meadows beyond. Freedom surged through her veins.

All those weeks cooped up in her room, with a dark cloud over her head while she despaired over Nick, disappeared. Once again she felt alive.

When the ranch was a speck in the distance, she pulled Bowie to a trot. *Should I go and see?* By this time the mustangs would have moved on to lusher pastures at the farthest reaches of the ranch and beyond. Never one to turn down an adventure, Chancy pressed Bowie forward in the direction of Wild Horse Lake. The last location the mustangs had grazed before she and Nick had captured Snowbar.

When she reached the rocky terrain of the lake, she knew she was right. There were no fresh tracks, only molded hoof-prints baked into the ground from earlier in the summer. The grass here was wilted, brown and yellows stalks crisp from the sun crunched under Bowie's hooves.

Disappointment flooded her system as she reined her horse to return to the ranch.

Her dark mood was short lived. Once out in the open, under the sunlight, it was impossible to remain upset. There will be others, she reasoned. Just not any as special as Snowbar. His rare markings made him unique, but he was a wild animal, she had to remember.

The next morning, when Chancy stepped into the kitchen, her mother handed her a cup of hot coffee before she sat at the table. Surprised, Chancy looked at her parents. Their faces had matching expressions of expectation.

"Chancy, I can't afford to send to many men out in search of Nick. Would you be willing to ride with Jed the next few days, see if you can help him pick up the boy's trail?"

Chancy's stomach fluttered. A chance to find Nick and see him one last time.

"Yes, Pa. I'd be glad to help," she answered, excited at the prospect.

"I'd suggest riding over to Lake County today. See if he stopped in any of the small towns along the way for supplies for his journey. It's a place to start at least."

***

Chancy saddled two horses, Bowie for herself, and a fresh ranch horse for Jed to use.

"Thanks for doing this," Jed said, entering the barn.

"I don't mind at all," Chancy replied. She led the horses outside into the sunlight. Jed followed, and they mounted the horses without further conversation.

Chancy relaxed in the saddle. The warmth of the sun made her sleepy when Jed's deep voice woke her.

"This is beautiful country. It's wild and untamed in a different way from Boston. There, the world is full of browns and grays, where here the land seems full of blues, and greens. So vivid and untouched. I can see why Nick would like it here."

"I couldn't imagine living anywhere else. My parents wanted me to move to Omaha to finish my studies. I visited there earlier this summer. I'd never felt so out of place and lost in my life. Everything is so constricted, there are so many rules to follow, and so many people. I thought I was going to suffocate there."

"Yes, in the east the rules are much different. It would be scandalous for me to ride alone with you as we are now. Your reputation would be tarnished," Jed stated matter of fact.

Chancy laughed at this. "I don't think I'll ever go back if I can avoid it."

They rode a short time longer before Chancy pulled up her horse. "Ma sent a lunch with me if you'd like to give the horses a break. We should reach town in another hour or so if we pick up the pace."

"Sure, I'll never turn down a meal with a pretty girl." Jed smiled and gave her a wink.

Chancy ignored the heat that covered her cheeks. Jed was as handsome as Nick, but didn't make her heart skip a beat in the way Nick did. She dismounted and pulled the sack her mother had packed for them out of her saddlebag.

Jed took her horse's reins and led them to a tree, out of the sun and tied them to a branch. While he was tending the horses, she set out the sandwiches and cookies her mother had sent, along with apple slices and beef jerky. There was more than enough food for two people.

Chancy sat in the grass and took a bite of her sandwich. Jed joined her moments later and reached for a cookie. He gave her a boyish grin before biting into one of her mother's famous cookies.

"Your mother is a wonderful cook," he said, reaching for his sandwich.

"I must agree." Chancy smiled.

"You remind me of my sister. She's a young lady who knows what she wants and strives to achieve her goals on her terms. I could see you both getting along grand."

"Nick's only mentioned her a few times. What does she do in Boston? Nick said she's a few years my elder," Chancy asked, her curiosity of Nick's family piqued.

"Elsie? Oh, she's quite the little wildcat. Of the three of

us Stone siblings, she takes after my father the most. Much to his chagrin, I'm sure. He'd like his sons proficient in the world of banking, but Elsie has a head for numbers unlike anything I've ever seen. She's a keen mind. Her only setback is she's a woman. I don't consider this a problem myself, but my father won't let her work in the bank. So, she's become a teacher instead."

Chancy thought of her own family situation. Her father, she knew had high hopes for his sons.

But since they had passed on, that left Chancy to uphold the Mallory traditions. "I think Elsie and I would be very good friends."

Jed grinned at her. "I think you're right."

They traveled at a steady trot until they reached town. To Chancy's dismay, the trip was in vain. No one from the mercantile to the blacksmith had seen a boy of Nick's description pass through town as of late.

"He must have traveled north instead of further west," Chancy said. Her hopes had been high to have had word of Nick in town.

"It was worth a try at least," Jed replied. His features were drawn and tired.

"My mother sent enough food for several days, we could ride north and see if anyone has seen him." Chancy didn't mind the travel, especially if there'd be word of Nick.

"No, I don't want to keep you away from the ranch any longer than necessary. When Nick wants to be found, he'll send word. Let's just go back."

Chancy didn't argue. Jed was right. When Nick wanted to have his whereabouts known, he'd send word. Otherwise, they could search for days and weeks and never hear word of him. The ache in her heart remained as she and Jed began their journey back to the ranch.

CHAPTER NINETEEN

Nick combed the last of the cockle-burs from Snowbar's long, black, tail. The horse gleamed in the morning sunlight. Satisfied with his work, he saddled and bridled the mustang. Today, he would ride the colt onto the Mallory's property.

With Bones excited woofs at his horse's heels, Nick nudged the colt into a ground eating trot, his own horse on a lead following close behind. He shifted in the saddle. Memories of the last time he and Chancy had spoken still haunted him. The look of deceit in her eyes when he'd told her he was leaving never strayed far from his mind.

If it weren't for Chancy, he would have been long on his way to making his own dreams come true. Instead, guilt-ridden when he'd spied the colt, he couldn't continue on. Not until he made things right between them once more. Somehow, some-way, Chancy Mallory had worked her way into his heart.

The Mallory ranch was in sight. Nick rode past a vast herd of grazing cattle. This time of year, the grasses dried to a honey colored hue. The fragrant woodsy smell of baked sagebrush wafted under his nose as he passed by.

"Land of the gods," Nick murmured under his breath. The ranch lay just beyond the bluffs he now closed in on. He found himself relaxed when something dawned on him. This feels like home. A touch of homesickness overcame him then, for this would never truly be his home. His family, parents and sibling were located back east.

Alma Mallory had questioned him about his parents and a nag of guilt had him sending off a note not long after. Only, there had been no reply in return. He'd shut the hurt out of his mind at the time. Haven't I hurt them by leaving as I did? He knew the truth of those words. His mother would have been devastated with his disappearance.

Now, minutes from the barn, Nick's heart thundered beneath his shirt. He was both excited and anxious about seeing Chancy again. Would he be able to redeem himself in her eyes with this gift? If not, then time, as his mother had told him in the past, healed all hurts. There was no turning back now, the barn entrance loomed in front of him.

Chancy sat at the table, coffee in hand, listening to her father tell Jed yet another story of the ranch's history. He'd be leaving, to return back east in the next few days. Since Nick's departure, no one had seen him. The land was too vast to keep the ranch hands searching for him day in and day out. The men had scoured the outlaying towns with no success. Nick had rode off the property and disappeared into the wind.

The Mallory ranch was the last attempt Jed had of finding his brother. Jim had promised if word did arise of Nick's whereabouts, they'd send him a letter right away. It wasn't the best way to give Nick the news, but it would have to do.

"Excuse me," Chancy stood and left the table. The men hadn't seemed to notice her at all, so deep in conversation over the economics of ranching. Nick's brother was an accountant at his father's bank in Boston. A very prominent one. She'd overheard her father telling her ma, Jed gave him some sound advice for the future in upcoming decisions he needed to make for the ranch.

Chancy set her plate on the counter and walked to the window. She glanced in the direction of the barn. What she saw stopped her short. "Nick! Oh my gosh, Pa, it's Nick—he's back. With Snowbar!"

Without waiting to find out if her father and Jed followed, she raced out the front door. She pulled her boots on with haste then ran down the drive. Not bothering to care if her mother became upset with her.

Nick stood beside Snowbar. The majestic mustang stood docile, his ears pricked forward while he watched her advance. His coat gleamed in the sunlight. Silver mane and tail glistened.

Tears sprang to Chancy's eyes. Could it be? Was this a dream where she'd wake up to disappointment once more?

Her questions were answered, when the black and white floppy-eared pup she so loved, rounded the corner of the barn and barked in her direction. "Bones!" The pup was quick to demand her attention. He hopped up and placed his paws on her chest. "You silly boy, did you miss me?" She giggled and ran her hand down his back. He rewarded her with a generous lick of his tongue across her cheek.

"Well, are you going to say something?" Nick asked, concern written across his face.

Chancy blinked back tears and swallowed the acorn sized lump lodged in her throat. "You brought Snowbar back." The tears broke loose and flowed freely down her face. Uncertain what to do she stood in place and wiped the wetness from her cheeks with the back of her hand.

She wanted to go to him and wrap her arms around him, lay her head against his chest. But some invisible line remained between them, and she was helpless to do anything but stare. She raised her chin and looked him in the eye. A flash of hurt crossed his face from the distance. Instead of Nick's warm arms, she hugged Bones tight and buried her cheek in his soft fur.

"Thank you," she said moments later, standing and stepping toward him. Nick took a step toward her until they were mere inches apart. Chancy smiled then. It was so good seeing him again.

She raised her hand and placed it over his heart. She could feel the thud, thud, thud of each heartbeat through the fabric.

"I've missed you," she whispered and dared a glance in his eyes.

"I've missed you too, Chancy."

He pulled her into his arms and held her tight, his chin resting on her head.

"Bringing me Snowbar is the nicest thing anyone's ever done for me," she muttered into his chest.

"When I left, I never expected to return so soon. I came

across the herd, spotted Snowbar, and I knew I had to bring him to you. He's your horse."

"Well look what we have here." Jim's voice boomed behind her.

"Brother—I've been searching for you." Jed's voice was solemn.

"Jed, what brought you out west?" Nick stepped away from Chancy and offered his hand to his brother.

"Come on now, you can do better than that." Jed pulled Nick into a hug. The brothers stood for several moments locked in an embrace.

"I've come with news," Jed pulled away. "And unfortunately it's not good." Jed's face paled, his features dim.

"What's happened, is everyone okay?" Nick's voice was low and strained.

Chancy stepped to her father's side. The news was heartbreaking. Nick would be devastated when he heard.

"Mother is gone," Jed's words were just above a whisper. "Father asked me to come west and tell you in person. She passed a little over a month ago. Doc thought it was some kind of cancer, she went quick and peaceful in her sleep."

Chancy dared a glance at Nick. A tear stained his cheek. She saw a rainbow of emotions cross his face, pain, anger, agony. She wished she could hug him. A small consolation for his loss, but was unsure of herself.

"I see," Nick replied after several moments. He wiped his face with a handkerchief pulled from his back pocket.

"Father said if it wasn't too much trouble, he'd like for you to return home, and pay your respects. But if not, if you're too busy here, he thought mother would understand. It sounds like you've built a life for yourself out here already."

Nick glanced at his brother, pain etched in his tanned features. "I'll return to Boston with you."
He then walked away from the group, shoulders sagging, gait stiff and slow.

Chancy hurt for him. She couldn't imagine the kind of

pain he must be in over the loss of his mother. She shuddered from the chill which had snaked up her back. She turned and glanced at Snowbar. Her heart leaped in her chest. She had her horse back. But when she should have felt great excitement, heartbreak suffocated her.

She walked to the colt and stroked his shoulder. He stood still and accepted her touch. "Hey boy, remember me?" She lay her hand flat in front of his nostrils so he could smell her scent. His nose was soft as silk. *Snowbar's mine for keeps,* the thought should have had her dancing from the rooftops, so why did a dark shadow cross her soul? Was it because of Nick, and the news he'd just received? The look of pain on Nick's face had devastated her.

Nick and Jed had disappeared toward the house, Bones close behind. They would need to finish making plans for their return trip. Nick would once again be out of her reach. Losing him for a second time seemed so much more painful.

"That's quite some boy, isn't he?" Jim nodded in the direction Nick and Jed had just left in.

"Yes, Pa, he is," she responded.

"I always thought he'd make a hell of a rancher. I hope once he gets his family life in order, he'll make it back here and pursue his dreams. I think he'd be very successful."

"I couldn't agree more." Chancy left her father's side then, with Snowbar's reins in her hand, she walked him into the corral. She wanted to feel the power, the smooth gaits beneath her.

"Good boy," she cooed, closing the corral gate behind her. With slow, smooth movements, she placed her boot in the stirrup and pulled herself into the saddle. Nick had worked his magic with this colt. He was attentive and obedient to her every cue. Her heart was full of respect for Nick and what he'd done for her. *How will I ever be able to repay him for this kindness?*

That evening at the dinner table, Nick joined them halfway through the meal. When he sat beside her, Chancy could see the whites of his eyes were bloodshot, his nose raw, and his lips chapped.

Her heart ached for him. Reaching under the table she placed her hand on his knee and gave a gentle squeeze. Nick gave her a half-hearted smile in return.

Later that night, while in her room, Chancy glanced out her window. A full white moon showed bright against the backdrop of darkness. A deep restlessness stirred in her soul. She wanted to go out and see the horses. See Snowbar. The mustang beckoned her.

Something had changed in her heart with Nick's return. Though she was thankful for him bringing the horse back to her, it didn't seem right to keep the wild animal. She never thought she'd feel this way, but keeping the mustang in captivity broke her heart. Grabbing a shawl, she stepped out of her room and made her way out of the house.

The barn was quiet, just the occasional swish of a tail, snort, or pawing at the ground. Chancy made her way to Bowie's stall. The mare stepped forward and nudged her mistress with her head.

"Hey, girl. I'm happy to see you too." Chancy rubbed the horse between the eyes. Snowbar they'd left outside in the corral. He'd never been exposed to a stall or its confines before. She left Bowie and wandered outside to check on how he was doing this night.

In the moonlight, Nick stood against the rails, chin resting on crossed arms. "Hello," Chancy greeted him, settling in beside him.

"Couldn't sleep?" Nick turned his face toward her. Heat radiated off of his body against her arm. Being so close to him was distracting enough, but tonight her feelings were elevated. The blood coursed through her veins and she would swear she could hear a buzzing in her ears.

"No—you too?"

"I've just been thinking about my mother. How things would be if I'd never of left. I think deep down, things wouldn't be all that different. My course in life is so different from everyone else in my family. I wasn't meant to work as a banker. If I return with Jed, I worry my father will try to coerce me back into the family business. I don't think I can handle sitting inside all day behind a desk."

Chancy remained quiet by his side, unsure how to respond. She didn't want Nick to go back east either, but would never speak this admission aloud.

"Snowbar sure is a good horse." He changed the subject. "He's a beauty. I've never seen anything like him."

Chancy looked over the rail at the mustang. The white of his coat shone bright in the moonlight.

He stood at the far corner of the corral, alert and ever watchful. Her heart did a little somersault. Her mind had been clouded with worry over her thoughts all afternoon. One of the reasons she'd come out tonight.

"There's something I need to talk with you about, Nick," she began. Her mouth became dry, and a knot formed in her stomach. *Can I tell him?* She didn't want to upset him any further. With all the distressing news he'd received today, she hated to add to the load.

"What's wrong, Chancy?" Nick looked her in the eye, his gaze full of worry.

"I think we should let Snowbar free. So he can keep the mustang legacy alive. He's a rare find, his colts will be strong and beautiful like him. I hate the thought of keeping him captive here. He's so wild and free." She paused, tapping her fingers on the rough wood of the rail. "I never thought I'd feel this way." She waited for angry words to erupt from his mouth. He'd put his plans on hold to bring back her horse and now she wanted to let the mustang back into the wild.

Instead of the angry words she'd expected, Nick pulled her to him. His lips were soft, inquisitive on hers. She wanted more. She wrapped her hand around the back of his neck, his hair soft and silky between her fingers. The kiss intensified until they were both breathless.

"Should we let him go tonight?" Nick asked her.

"Yes, let's do it now. Together." She reached for his hand

and pulled him with her back inside the barn. Chancy grabbed a halter from a hook at the entrance.

"Are you sure you want to do this, Chancy? I don't want you to regret this in the morning."

Nick's gaze had a serious intent, a hint of worry about his eyes.

"I've never been more sure of anything in my life." She returned his gaze. She'd never been more confident about any decision she'd ever made. She smiled in hopes to calm his fears and reached for his hand. She brought his fingers to her cheek. The calloused rough exterior made her skin tingle.

They stood in silence, locked in one another's gaze. Nick was the first to glance away.

"Let me pen Bones in the barn so he doesn't follow." Nick disappeared into one of the stalls, Bones followed. He quickly stepped out and shut the dog inside.

"I'll be back soon boy, you stay here." He stepped back from the stall and turned to Chancy,

"Okay, you ready to go?"

"Yes," she answered.

Hand in hand, they led Snowbar across the meadow in the shadows of the moonlight. Chancy had no second thoughts, no regrets. This felt right in her heart.

They walked for some time before Nick spoke. "I wonder if my mother is looking down on me from heaven right now?"

Chancy was surprised by his question. She wasn't known for her words of knowledge. Especially when it came to death. Instead, she gave his hand a gentle squeeze. "I'm sure she is. My ma says my older brothers all watch over me from above. I don't remember much about them, but their spirits live in my heart.

"Thanks, Chancy," Nick said.

"For what?" His words confused her.

"For understanding. For not telling me how I should feel. I'll admit to you only, but I've never felt more lost in my life. I don't know what to do."

His hand quivered in hers. They stopped among a cluster

of trees. Chancy leaned forward and kissed his cheek.

"I'll be here for you."

Nick turned, a question in his gaze.

"When you leave, and I know you have to, I'll be here waiting for you. However long it takes, Nick. I just want you to remember that." She stared at the ground.

His fingers lifted her chin, so she was forced to look at him once more. He kissed her with gentleness, then pulled away.

"I'll be back for you, Chancy. I don't want to lose you."

"You won't lose me, Nick." Her eyes now watered and she sniffed to hold the tears in. She wanted to tell him she loved him, but couldn't. The words were stuck in her mind, but she wasn't able to bring them to her lips. She didn't want to add any further burdens or guilt to his conscience with that kind of declaration.

"Well the time is here." He ran his hand down Snowbar's sleek neck. "Do you want to say goodbye?"

"Yes," her answer came out barely audible. A lump the size of an apple was stuck in her throat and the tears now flowed freely. She hugged the colt's neck. He smelled as only a horse could. She breathed deep, not wanting to ever forget. Snowbar shook his head and pawed the ground.

"Anxious, boy?" Chancy smiled through her tears. "You go and find yourself some good mares now. Maybe someday, when the time is right, God will grant me the privilege of owning one of your offspring." With one last pat to his shoulder, she stepped away.

"You ready for me to let him go?" Nick asked again. His features raw with grief, he wiped his eyes while he stared at her.

"Yes, do it." She swallowed hard. Nick removed the halter from Snowbar and stepped to her side. The horse remained still. "Is he going to go?" Chancy choked through her tears.

"Just wait, he'll realize he's free in a minute."

Time stood still while they watched and waited. Snowbar tossed his head to the side. Then with a half rear, he bolted off into the night.

"Goodbye...," Chancy whispered. Her shoulders shook with force. Nick wrapped her in his arms and held her tight against his chest. She sobbed, unable to control her emotions any longer. When she noticed Nick trembled against her, she held him tighter. They had to comfort one another for all the losses, big and small, they were forced to endure. Life for them would go on, and together they'd make it a good one.

Sometime later, Chancy couldn't be sure of the time, the moon had moved, and the sky glittered in the lights of a multitude of stars. "Nick?" she shook his shoulder. They'd fallen asleep on the ground, wrapped in each other's arms.

"Wh—what?" his voice croaked, still groggy with sleep.

"We need to go back to the ranch. It will be morning soon," she answered softly.

Nick raised himself onto his elbows, long limbs stretched out before him. A cool breeze blew across the land. An early reminder that soon fall would be upon them. Summer was coming to an end, the subtleness of the changes would be lost on the average soul.

"This is my favorite time of night. When the earth is so tranquil. After I left the ranch a couple of weeks back, I'd wake out on the range this time of morning and just sit and watch and listen. I'd never felt so at peace like I did then. Like I do now."

Chancy searched the darkness. What he said made sense. Her heart was calm, anything seemed possible.

CHAPTER TWENTY

Nick and Chancy returned to the ranch house. After a chaste kiss goodnight, he'd watched the front door close quietly behind her. He wasn't sure how long he stood there after she left. His mind was in a fog. Today, he was to leave with Jed. They would return to Boston, so he could see his family and pay his respects to his mother. Then, as he had promised Chancy earlier in the night, he would return.

Bones crawled onto his chest, after he'd stretched out on his cot. "Bones—no boy. I don't need your kisses." The dog ignored his pleas and swiped his other cheek with his wet tongue. "Ugg," Nick despaired. A dog's love was absolute, and at times, a little sloppy. Nick covered his face with his arm and Bones burrowed against his side. It was some time before sleep overcame him.

Nick awoke the next morning to the crow of the rooster. The hands were already out on the range. Their day's work began before sunrise each morning. He'd slept in. The knowledge of this made him cringe with guilt.

He threw the covers off and dressed. Bones stretched with great animation then sat beside the door in wait for his master. He'd be back for his belongings later. They were still in the pack next to his bed. With Bones beside him, Nick made his way to the ranch house. The time for goodbyes had arrived.

Mrs. Mallory, let him in the front door and led him into the dining room. "I'm afraid Chancy's still asleep in her bed," the woman said ahead of him. "This is not like her at all."

"Oh," Nick replied, as a slow heat crept up his neck.

"I'm here, Ma," Chancy said, brushing past her mother and taking her seat at the table. Nick took the seat beside her and placed his hands on the table. All eyes were on them.

"Chancy, do you have something you'd like to tell us?" Jim asked, his brows drawn together in a frown.

Chancy glanced at him. Her face was haggard from their late night. Dark circles shadowed her eyes.

"The men told me this morning the colt is missing. There were no signs of forced escape, so it appears that someone has released him."

Chancy cleared her throat. "Nick and I let him go. Last night." She stared at her plate.

"Is that so," Jim replied and looked at Nick.

"It was her decision, sir. I did help her. It seemed the right thing to do."

Jim nodded and took a sip of his coffee. Alma and Jed remained quiet in their seats.

"I'll be ready within the hour, Jed. I know you're probably ready to get back to Boston, and back to your job."

"Not necessarily, Nick. I've found that I've enjoyed my time here immensely. But I must agree with you, we will need to go soon. The return trip to Boston will be long."

Nick stood from the table. His appetite was gone. "Chancy, care to walk to the barn and help me saddle the horses?"

Chancy stood, her chair scraping across the floor. "Yes, I think I would."

No words were spoken by anyone when they left the room. Chancy walked by his side, matching his pace on the way to the barn. He turned his head; his heart dropped to his stomach when he saw the tears streaming down her face once more. There was no easy way to do this.

"I'll saddle Jed's horse." Chancy pulled away from him and beat him inside the barn by a full stride. They saddled the horses in silence. Nick gave her time to gather her emotions. He had something to ask of her before he left.

Horses saddled and ready, Nick needed to speak with Chancy now, before his brother showed up and was ready to leave. He walked over to Bowie's stall and rubbed the mare's neck.

"Chancy, come here, I have something I need to ask of you."

She tied Jed's horse to the hitching rail and walked over to him. Bones sat panting at Nick's feet.

He couldn't take the dog. Bones would be a hindrance on the way east, and it would kill him if something happened to his beloved pup. The only answer was to ask Chancy to keep him. It would serve as a token of trust that he would return.

"I have something I need to ask of you while I'm away." Her chin raised, her eyes glittered in the light, but she didn't cry.

"What's wrong?" she asked. He noticed only a slight crack in her voice.

"Would you keep Bones for me?" He noticed her sharp intake of breath, but continued on. "I will return, Chancy. For you and Bones, I swear I will come back."

He pulled her to his chest and gave her a soul numbing kiss. He felt the connection clear to his toes. He would have never ended the union, but the sound of his brother clearing his throat behind him pulled him up short.

"Sorry to interrupt. I was going to get my horse." Jed wore an amused smile on his lips.

"Your horse is ready." Chancy sucked in a breath at his side.

They watched as Jed took the reins to his mount. "I'll wait outside," he said on his way through the entrance.

"I'll do it, Nick. I love Bones, he'll be no trouble at all."

"Thanks, Chancy. That's a huge relief to my mind." He leaned in and gave her a quick peck on the lips. He wasn't good at goodbyes, and this one was tearing his heart to pieces.

"Your brother is waiting." Chancy reminded him, a sad smile on her face.

Nick nodded and reached for his mount's reins. It took all his strength to step out of the barn and into the daylight. Jed had already mounted and talked with Jim and Alma.

"Hold my horse while I go fetch my things?" he asked

Chancy.

She reached for the reins and smiled. His boots were heavier than a bucket of mud. Each step was a struggle, but soon he reached the bunkhouse and gathered his belongings. A smile remained plastered on Chancy's face when he returned.

"Keep Bones with you the next few days. I don't want him to chase after me and follow my scent."

"I'll do it, Nick." She handed him his reins and reached down to grab the dog's collar.

"I've sent you with enough food to hold you over till you reach the train station," Alma spoke up. "You boy's take care now, you hear? It can be dangerous out there."

"Yes, Mrs. Mallory, we'll keep our eyes peeled for danger. This is the wild west." Jed chuckled at his own humor.

"We'll watch ourselves, Mrs. Mallory, don't you fret," Nick spoke, but his eyes were glued on Chancy. He wanted to kiss her one last time, but the time for such things had passed. Jed had already spurred his horse forward, dust clouds rising under his horse's hooves.

"Goodbye, Chancy." His tongue was thick, and his mouth dry.

"Goodbye." She stood rigid, her face grim. Nick could tell she struggled to stay composed.

"Take care, boys," Jim called out with a wave.

Nick turned his horse and nudged him forward. Dare he glance behind one last time? No, it would be too painful seeing the tears on Chancy's face.

CHAPTER TWENTY-ONE

Through blurred eyelashes, Chancy watched Nick ride out of her life. *He will be back, he will be back,* she chanted in her mind. She took a few hesitant steps forward. I can't let him leave without this.

She grasped the wooden horse between her fingers.

Heart pounding, she began to run. Bones followed at her side, barking wildly. "Nick—Nick... stop!" she cried. She continued to run; her chest hurt, but she ignored the hitch in her side and increased her speed.

He didn't look back. Can't he hear me? He was moments from being out of sight. Panicked and out of breath, she stopped. Her sides heaved, and she bent forward in pain. It was over. He hadn't heard her and now he was gone. Gone, until the next time she saw him and when would that be? Weeks from now, months from now? Maybe even years from now.

Chancy sank to her knees, her grief was so great. Why did it matter if she didn't give him the relic? He'd given her his most loved possession, his pet dog, Bones. What had she given him? Maybe her heart, but she wanted him to have something solid, something he could grasp in his hand and remember her by.

"Chancy?"

She jerked her head at the sound of the familiar voice. "Nick?" Her heart once again thundered, a momentary dizziness shook her from the rush of blood pounding in her skull. She stood, still in awe that he was standing before her.

Bones jumped around at his legs, wanting to play. Nick ignored him and reached for Chancy's shoulder. "I heard you call my name. What's wrong?" His face was etched with concern.

"I—I forgot to give you this." Chancy showed him the toy running horse. It was smooth from years of handling.

"This is your special horse. The one that was once your brothers'. You can't let me take this from you."

"I want you to. You've put Bones in my care. When I see him, and play with him, I'll always think of you. But you have nothing of me. Nothing to remind you of me."

A smile jerked at the corner of Nick's lip. "Oh, Chancy, everything reminds me of you. From the prettiest wildflower, to the spirit of the wild horses. I see you everywhere. You're not someone who's so easy to forget."

Chancy quivered when he kissed her lips. She grabbed his shoulders and pulled him to her. Her kiss was fierce and possessive. She wanted to brand him with her taste. She'd not let him forget her.

Ever.

"Here, take this. Bring it back to me, you hear?" Chancy stuffed the wooden horse into his hand.

"I promise to return this to you, Chancy." He kissed her one last time.

It was the most haunting kiss she'd ever experience. A shadow passed over her heart, but she brushed away her superstitions. Nick said he would return, and she believed him.

"Okay, well I guess this is goodbye for the last time," she croaked.

"Don't feel bad, I'm not so good with goodbyes myself." With a grin he squeezed her shoulder and stepped away.

"Goodbye, Chancy," he said once he'd mounted his horse again.

"Goodbye." She smiled, while holding Bones in her arms.

Nick tipped his hat in her direction, a breathtaking smile on his lips. His horse tossed its head and pawed at the ground. Nick loosened the reins, and the horse bolted forward. Chancy waved goodbye. She waved until her arm was tired.

When Nick could no longer be seen she turned toward the ranch house. A peaceful sensation

came over her and she smiled.

"He'll be back, Bones. Just wait and see."

To be continued...

Author Bio: L.B.Shire

L.B. Shire has been writing stories for as long as she can remember. She's always looking for a good horse story and if one can't be found, she makes one up herself.

When not writing or researching, L.B. enjoys spending time with family, spoiling her pampered pony, and, of course, reading anything that is set before her! She currently resides on the West Coast in a sleepy little mountain town. There, in the midst of all that beauty, she plans her characters' next adventures.

Made in the USA
Las Vegas, NV
07 June 2021

24333969R00097